Margaret Mary Smith Cook

Women's Suffrage

Margaret Mary Smith Cook

Women's Suffrage

ISBN/EAN: 9783743353770

Manufactured in Europe, USA, Canada, Australia, Japa

Cover: Foto ©ninafisch / pixelio.de

Manufactured and distributed by brebook publishing software
(www.brebook.com)

Margaret Mary Smith Cook

Women's Suffrage

WOMEN'S SUFFRAGE.

BY

MRS. ASHTON DILKE

WITH INTRODUCTION BY

WM. WOODALL, M.P.

London:
SWAN SONNENSCHEIN AND CO.
PATERNOSTER SQUARE.
1885.

UNWIN BROTHERS, THE GRESHAM PRESS, CHILWORTH AND LONDON.

CONTENTS.

	PAGE
INTRODUCTION	11

CHAP.
I. REPLY TO HABITUAL OBJECTIONS—PHYSICAL AND MENTAL	19
II. REPLY TO HABITUAL OBJECTIONS—WOULD WOMEN BE LESS WOMANLY?	26
III. REPLY TO HABITUAL OBJECTIONS—EXPEDIENCY	36
IV. THE HARDSHIPS OF EXCLUSION	48
V. PARTY POLITICS	59
VI. WOMEN'S GRIEVANCES	65
VII. RIGHTS ALREADY OBTAINED	83
VIII. A LIMITED DEMAND FOR JUSTICE	87

APPENDICES—

		PAGE
I.	Reply of Mr. Disraeli to the Memorial of Women's Suffrage, April 29, 1873	103
II.	Sir Stafford Northcote's Speech, April 7th	103
III.	Mr. Joseph Cowen's Speech, June, 1884	104
IV.	Mr. Herbert Spencer	106
V.	Mrs. Henry Fawcett	106
VI.	Women's Suffrage in the Middle Ages	107
VII.	Mr. Gladstone on the Women's Disabilities Removal Bill, May 3, 1871	108
VIII.	Mr. Fawcett's Speech, Oct. 13, 1884	110
IX.	The Bishop of Carlisle	111
X.	The Agar-Ellis Case	112
XI.	Professor Lindsay, D.D.	115
XII.	Mr. Courtney, M.P.	116
XIII.	Rev. Canon Kingsley	117
XIV.	Lord John Manner's Speech, March 24, 1884	118
XV.	Female Employment in England	119
XVI.	Colonel King-Harman's Speech, June, 1884	121

INDEX 123

WOMEN'S SUFFRAGE.

INTRODUCTION.

THE Parliament of 1880, prorogued and waiting only the final stroke of dissolution, has had, like all its predecessors, a chequered fortune. It has disappointed many confident expectations, but it has distinguished itself historically in one notable particular. It has dealt with the complex problems of parliamentary reform with an effect which for courage and completeness dwarfs the achievements of 1832 and 1867. It has gone far to reconcile the practice with the theory of the English constitution. Mr. Puff remarked that "where they do agree on the stage, their unanimity is wonderful." But even the *omnes* of the stage directions is outdone when Liberals and Conservatives compete for the credit of enfranchisement, from the moment that issue is clearly inevitable. The poor denizen of the Irish hovel; the groom or hind for whom shelter is found as part of his weekly wage; the humble cotter so needy, or it may be so thriftless, that he has to rely upon the Poor Law when sickness calls for medical aid; the illiterate for whom an elaborate special process of voting has to be maintained—all have been effectively admitted within the constitution, and recognized as having, equally with the wealthiest, an interest in the good government of the commonwealth. The civil servants, and even the policemen—whose neutrality formerly was regarded as essential during the fierce conflicts of election time—have had their title admitted by the competing leaders.

But, in the fervour of enfranchisement, one conspicuous exception has been made, one glaring disability remains, one anomaly survives to prevent the closing of the current chapter of parliamentary reform.

If it be true, that the onus of proof has properly rested on those who have in the past opposed enfranchisement, it will be conceded that this obligation rests with peculiar force on those who oppose the claims urged on behalf of persons who, satisfying all the other conditions required by the law, are debarred on the ground of sex alone.

Women have to contribute equally with men to local and imperial taxation, though in regard to the latter they are denied any voice as to levying it or in its expenditure; they have no exemption from the obligation to obey the laws, though they have no part in the making of them. In spite of the nonsense talked about women's sphere, it is true of the great majority of women as of men, that they who will not work neither shall they eat. They do work, often fettered and cruelly handicapped. Women who earn a separate livelihood may be counted by millions, and each

INTRODUCTION. 13

census testifies to the fact that these numbers increase decade by decade at something like the rate of 30 per cent. Triumphing over all impediments, women have attained the very highest rank in art, in literature, and in the science of teaching. They have overcome the prejudices which excluded them from the advantages of the Universities, and from the learned professions. In every form of public duty women have rendered conspicuous service. What an aching void would be created were it possible to efface the female toilers in the activities of temperance, religious, emigration, or reformatory work !

They have had official status from time immemorial in that they have been eligible for, and have served such offices as those of sheriff and churchwarden. The woman ratepayer has always voted for Poor Law Guardians; since 1870 she has voted also for School Boards, and has been eligible for election on both these bodies. Since 1867 in England, and more recently in Scotland, women have voted equally with men for the Town Councils; that right having, however, been limited to unmarried women by legal ruling in England, and by the express terms of the statute in Scotland. Four years ago the Queen in Council approved of the action of the Isle of Man legislature in conferring the parliamentary suffrage there on female freeholders. And, lastly, in the Bill, introduced last year, for constituting the Metropolitan Parliament, it was proposed that women householders should vote for members of the Council, might be themselves eligible for election, and might even fill, if called to that post, the most dignified position of all in the projected government for London!

Why not? Live we not under a constitution which has been interpreted and administered with amazing skill, resource, and fidelity, through a long period of unexampled national activity, and over crises which have shaken every other European power? Can it be said that there has been any want of capacity for government manifested during this long and eventful reign, albeit the ruler has been—a woman?

If, then, the truth of this recital be admitted, <u>if women have shown aptitude for vocations so diverse—from that of ministering angels in our hospitals, or of Poor Law Guardians, to the discharge of the highest functions of the State—why debar them from dropping a paper in the already familiar ballot-box once in three or four years along with the labourer who, in many thousands of cases, is dependent upon them for his subsistence?</u> The answers to this appeal are not wanting in force, though sometimes lacking in the quality of fairness. How far they are reasonable and consequent the reader of the following chapters may be left to judge. It will, at any rate, be felt instinctively that the duty of vindicating the claims urged on behalf of her sex devolves properly upon one who has been among the foremost in bravely battling for their recognition.

Not the least remarkable sign of progress in what has been called the Woman Question, is to be observed in the growth of a public sentiment in regard to the participation of women in certain special kinds of political and other public work. The contest which closed the electoral history of Woodstock the other day, is said to have been determined by the active part therein taken by the ladies who made their own the cause of the winning candidate. That this female zest for electioneering is no modern development, is clear from stories which have come down to us, like that of the Duchess of Devonshire and of her ungrudging devotion to the cause of Fox in the Westminster election. These instances, which might be multiplied to any extent, and from the experiences of any period, constitute only the comedy of the movement. In view of the fact that women are to-day taking their part in the constitution of Primrose Leagues and of Liberal Councils, it is almost startling to be reminded that seventeen years only have passed since sober people were shocked and pained by the appearance of women on public platforms as advocates of the claims of their sisterhood, and since it was said in Parliament that they had thereby disgraced themselves and their sex. The change marks the revolution which has taken place in the tone of party manners, under which we have seen the tranquil decorum of modern methods evolved out of the violence, the horse-play, and the debauchery of the times of Hogarth and of Mr. Pickwick. Women will be naturally more and more disposed to avail themselves of an improved condition of things they have done so much to bring about.

The name of Mr. Mill must ever be held in high and grateful regard as the pioneer of the parliamentary struggle for Women's Suffrage. He endeavoured to have "person" substituted for "man" in the Reform Act of 1867. Subsequently an appeal was heard by the Court of Common Pleas from women claiming the right of voting in reliance on the wording of the Statute, and of the provision in Lord Brougham's Act, that words importing the masculine gender shall be deemed and taken to include the feminine unless the contrary is expressly provided. The Court decided adversely, however, and since that time the question has been repeatedly before Parliament, with varying fortune. The last issue was taken under circumstances peculiarly embarrassing. The then Prime Minister declared that the success of the motion to enfranchise women would be fatal to the Franchise Bill, upon the passing of which the Liberal party was ardently resolved, though at a later date Mr. Gladstone generously justified the action of those who disregarded his menace. The division then demonstrated a new phase of the movement. There had never been a time when it had not the support of distinguished Conservatives. Mr. Russell Gurney was a teller with Mr. Mill in 1867. Lord Beaconsfield, Lord Iddesleigh, and Lord John Manners long ago declared their adhesion.[1] In the Parliament of 1874 Mr. Forsyth, Conservative member for Marylebone, had charge of the Bill. But in 1883, out of 132 voting for the resolution submitted by

[1] See Appendices I. and II.

Mr. Hugh Mason, 19 only were Conservatives. In 1884 this number had swollen to 96. The proposed clause was rejected by a majority of 136, in consequence of the severe pressure of the Government. But there voted in the majority not less than 104 Liberals who had signified their approval of the principle contended for, of whom more than one-half had signed a memorial to the Prime Minister to the effect that no measure of parliamentary reform would be complete and satisfactory which did not recognize the just claims of duly qualified women. There is therefore no room to doubt that had the chances of parliamentary time been more favourable, had it been possible to have taken another division under conditions free from the considerations which weighed with these 104 "Opportunist" opponents, most of them would have been found true to the cause which in one way or another they had approved. Had two-thirds of the number so voted, the adverse majority of 1884 would have disappeared.

The cause of Women's Suffrage is thus left to be numbered among the legacies which will devolve upon the new Parliament. Possessing their souls in patience, the friends of the movement will bate no jot of heart or hope. Conscious of the invincibility of the claim they have steadfastly urged, they have refrained from pressing it in season and out of season upon an over-burdened legislature. But they have good reason to be satisfied with the signs of substantial progress which abound on every hand. The evidence of petitions, of public meetings, large and small, of popular clubs and drawing-room gatherings: the education movement, the impassioned interest in social problems, and, above all, the testimony, the more conclusive because often reluctant, to the priceless value of the service rendered by devoted women in every direction, all combine to make irresistible the demand for the removal of their political disabilities.

To their confidence in the ultimate recognition of the justice of these claims may be traced the conspicuous moderation with which they are urged on the platform and in the press. Relying upon essential and abstract right, they have combined to secure "the Parliamentary Franchise for Women on the same conditions as it is, or may be, granted to men." But, in the following pages, as in everything which has been said and done by the principal friends of the English movement, this demand has been urged by appeals and demonstrations from experience, of its perfect reasonableness and expediency. In this respect they have been animated by the spirit which Mr. Mill evinced when, in commending his proposal to Parliament, he said—

"There is an important branch of expediency called justice, and justice—though it does not necessarily require that we should confer political functions on every one—does require that we should not capriciously and without cause withhold from one what we give to another."

CHAPTER I.

REPLY TO HABITUAL OBJECTIONS—PHYSICAL AND MENTAL.

IN discussing the question of "Women's Suffrage" in these pages, no attempt will be made to find novel arguments in favour of a change in the law that excludes women from political life, but rather an enumeration will be made of the more serious reasons alleged against it by its opponents, followed by the line of argument usually adopted by the friends of the movement. It will then be necessary to discuss the various suggestions made for altering the law, and to make some attempt to arrive at a satisfactory conclusion as to which suggestion it is best to support. The present state of the movement will also be touched upon, though space forbids the past history of so extensive an agitation being detailed.

The idea that women should not vote because they have less physical strength than men, seems extremely difficult to eradicate, and hardly a debate or public meeting can take place without some champion appearing to insist that because women are the weaker, therefore they are not to be considered capable of performing the duties of citizenship. That such an idea should have shot its roots down so deeply into men's minds, appears to show that the theory and meaning of constitutional government have not really, as yet, been properly grasped.

If the rule of the strongest is after all to prevail, if might is really right in the end, the very existence of parliaments seems threatened. It is because Englishmen have aimed at depriving those physically the strongest of the power they once held and misused, that constitutional government has gradually been built up for the protection of the weak. To pick out the weakest members of the community and refuse them representation, seems therefore entirely in contradiction of the theory of British institutions.

It was at one time urged, that were it not for centuries of seclusion and sedentary occupations, women would physically be equal to men, and that under altered conditions they might well become so; but their right to a vote seems to stand on a much firmer basis, if claimed for the weak as well as for the strong. This is one of the points on which men attempt to apply a test to women which they do not submit to themselves, for whether a man be blind or lame, undersized or crippled, he nevertheless votes.

It is urged that women are not called upon to fight for or to defend their country, that they cannot be soldiers, or sailors, or policemen.[1] But how many men

[1] See Appendix III.

in the British Isles fulfil these requirements? Do they all become soldiers and sailors in order to get a vote? It is well known that the great mass of our defenders are, by the fact of their enlistment, deprived of their votes.

As to the police, from their constant employment at home, they might be expected to take an intelligent interest in the government of their country; and as in most cases they live in their own homes, instead of massed together in barracks and war-ships like the soldiers and sailors, they would in a very large number of instances be entitled to a vote. But so jealous are Englishmen of the rule of the strongest being applied to themselves, that the police are forbidden under a very heavy penalty to enter the polling-booths and record their votes.[1] So women find they are refused votes because they do not, and indeed cannot, defend their country, and yet know that were they by disguise or other ruse to succeed in bearing arms, they would still find themselves excluded from participating in elections.

It is to the peaceable citizen and householder who stays at home, but pays for the army and navy and police force out of his own pocket, that the vote is entrusted. Women therefore claim that in this respect they are duly qualified. But they do more. They have always con-

[1] A Bill was introduced into the House of Commons by Mr. Coleridge Kennard at the latter end of the Session of 1885, with the object of removing the police disqualification; but it failed even to secure a second reading.

sidered the nursing of the sick and wounded and dying as their special privilege, and would be the last to claim a reward for it. But when men urge their power to wound and slay as a reason for giving them votes, surely the power of women to heal and tend and restore to health again should not be left out of account.

It certainly cannot be urged that women have *no* physical force, but only that it is somewhat less in quantity than that of men. Were it suggested that they should therefore have a smaller share of representation there would seem to be some logic in the argument; but when we see the vast amount of hard, toilsome physical work performed by women, it seems most illogical to treat them as if they had none.

On the intellectual question it is difficult to speak with as great precision, for even men hesitate to state positively that women are intellectually inferior to men, and therefore should be disfranchised. Those who do make this statement were certainly a much more formidable body twenty years ago than they are at present. Many of the old arguments against Women's Suffrage are becoming obsolete, and this question of the intellectual capacity of women stands undoubtedly in a very different position in consequence of the march of female education than it once did.

And the improved education of women has extended through all classes. The board schools in primary education, the high schools in middle-class education, and the women's colleges in the higher education, have all encouraged girls to compete with boys, and women with men on equal footing; and apart from the question of whether women should receive the same education as men, they have shown in an immense number of cases that they can pass the same examinations and take the same degrees.[1]

It must be remembered that in no sense can there be said to be an educational franchise in England. It is true that by an arrangement between the leaders of the two great parties, the University members of the House of Commons have been allowed to remain untouched by the Reform Bill of 1884–5, but even they are regarded by many as most anomalous. Elaborate arrangements are made at the polling-booths for giving effect to the unbiassed opinion of the illiterate voter, and in the outlying portions of Scotland, Ireland, and Wales, there are now included in the franchise large numbers of men who cannot speak a word of English, and who cannot read

---

[1] It may be interesting to give the latest instance of the educational attainments of women. "At the London University Matriculation, June, 1885, more than 1,100 candidates, male and female, entered for the examination. Of these 615 have been successful, and for the first time a lady heads the honours list, without being disqualified by age from receiving the exhibition of thirty pounds for two years. Two other ladies are among the prize receivers. In all thirty-five candidates have obtained either prizes or the number of marks qualifying for prizes, and eight of these are ladies. In the honours division, out of 136 candidates, 30 are ladies; and of the 615 successful candidates, 100 are ladies out of about 150 who entered for the examination."

or write any language at all. Certainly the women who now exercise the local votes can claim to be at least intellectually on an equality with these.

Again, it must be remembered, that it is not merely the book learning to be acquired in the silence of the study, that is supposed best to fit a man for the duties of citizenship. It is every-day intercourse of the freest kind with his fellow men, the general interchange of thought and opinion in the market and the workshop, the telling of grievances and the hearing of complaints, that helps a man to use his vote honestly for the good of the commonwealth and the improvement of society. And here, again, women are much more competent than formerly. They have much greater liberty to come and go; the number of women earning a livelihood outside their homes has vastly increased; being better educated, they know how to make better use of their eyes and ears; they more commonly read the newspapers and political pamphlets and periodicals, and have greater opportunities of exchanging ideas and forming opinions.

There is no better test of the consideration in which women are now held in the educational world, than the large amount of teaching that is in their hands. It is recognized that it is always best to entrust the teaching of girls to women, and that *young* boys fall naturally under their care also, so that the demand for well-educated, well-trained, female teachers for both public and private schools is large and increasing.

Another point to be remembered when considering the

intellectual capacities of women, is the great absence in their case of the special incentives to study that have been piled up for centuries for their more favoured brothers. Prizes, scholarships, exhibitions, money rewards of every kind have been accumulated by public and private benefactors for the advancement of the boys, whereas in some cases even those endowments that were originally intended for both boys and girls alike, have been absorbed by the male portion of the community, or have disappeared altogether.

The clever neat fingers of women specially fit them for those skilled trades for which technical training is a necessity. Yet go into any workhouse school or institution, where an attempt is made to teach the simpler industries as well as book learning, and we find there the boys are learning carpentering, boot-making, tailoring, or husbandry, according to their capacities and inclinations, while the girls are generally kept to sewing, which, however necessary as part of a woman's training, is the worst paid means of earning a livelihood.

In spite of all these disadvantages, some of which are slowly being remedied, and many others which it would be impossible to discuss here, it is readily admitted that the female portion of the community has advanced many steps towards equality with men in intellectual matters, and that to permanently exclude women from the franchise, on intellectual grounds only, is even less justifiable now than it was a quarter of a century back.

CHAPTER II.

REPLY TO HABITUAL OBJECTIONS—WOULD WOMEN BE LESS WOMANLY?

WOMEN are constantly urged to leave everything in the hands of men, and they will get whatever it is right for them to have. This argument is often used by those men who are themselves most eager to do justice to women and remedy their grievances, but who do not realize how small is the number of the chivalrous, and how vast are the armies of the selfish.

Since when have one or two women's questions, more particularly those relating to education and property, been dealt with in the Houses of Parliament? Exactly since the time that women have banded themselves together to ask for votes with which to do their own work. It may seem severe to say that the passing of these bills is but a sop thrown to women to keep them quiet, and yet, when it is seen with what reluctance these questions were attended to, it seems a justifiable assertion.

Women have suffered at least as much from the ignorance of men as to their real wants and wishes, as from any deliberate intention of legislating against them. It is now recognized, with regard to every class of men, that delegated representation means misrepresentation, and women are no exceptions. Surely it is the wearer, and not the shoemaker, that knows best where the shoe pinches. Women have suffered so bitterly from regulations intended for their benefit, that they now cry for a fair field and no favour, and are willing to abandon any little advantages they may possess, should they thereby secure the right to make their power felt.

Besides, Members of Parliament, however chivalrous, are but human. Their seats depend on the votes of their constituents, and it is to the cries of their constituents that they most readily respond. The pressure of time, and the multiplicity of demands for help in Parliament become yearly greater, and it is really no reproach to honourable members to say that they have no time to attend to such outsiders as the women are.

Before the first Reform Bill, the number of voters was so limited, that there was some pretence for saying that the voter represented his friends and neighbours who were less fortunate; but now that voters are reckoned by the million, it is a case of every man for himself.

Women have already proved to their own satisfaction how their wants are attended to if their arguments are backed by votes, as they find, since they have held the municipal vote, that town councillors have an ever-ready ear for women's grievances. So long as they have no votes, they can never be sure that even those liberties they possess are secure, nor that fresh disabilities and restrictions may not be slipped through Parliament before they have time to make use of that indirect influence that men assure them is so potent. There is a simplicity and a directness about their claim to a vote, with which to settle their own difficulties, that should recommend it to those who prefer going to the root of questions instead of merely scratching the surface.

But perhaps the most weighty argument which is used against granting a vote to women, is that it would cause a great loss of feminine charm and constitute a great injury to home life. These statements must be supposed to refer to the whole agitation for an improvement in the position and education of women, rather than to the very limited demand for a parliamentary vote. The point is one to discuss, for the opinions as to what constitutes "feminine charm" are so varied and contradictory.

There are undoubtedly many who think that the inevitable result of a woman earning her own living is to deteriorate her considerably, and to make her less desirable as a wife and mother of a family. There are, again, many who think that a woman is not truly womanly if she expresses opinions of her own, or is more deeply read in science, or literature, or languages than the men who surround her. But you cannot put back the hands of the clock, and it is idle to prevent a woman from obtaining education; indeed, many of those who most strongly object to her taking a part in political life, urge *political sphere.*

her to occupy herself at home in improving her own mind.

But education brings knowledge of the position of ※ women both at home and abroad. They see that in one country they are allowed rights over their property, in another rights over their children, that in another even some political rights are granted, and they soon learn that the only means men have devised for getting what they want is the vote.

The idea that an ignorant woman conducts her household best and rears her children most wisely is never now put forward. /Homes are best managed by women who combine education with knowledge of the world, common sense, and a feeling of responsibility. When you give a vote to such women they will undoubtedly continue to make use of these qualities in their homes as well as at the polling-booths./

It is, to some extent, true that women cannot well combine the earning of their livelihood with home life. But those who wish to put a vote into her hands do not insist that every woman should earn her own livelihood. They only wish that the large number of women who are inevitably obliged to work, should do so under the best possible conditions; that, as unskilled labour means starvation, or the workhouse, or the streets, to hundreds of thousands of women, they should be enabled, while young enough to learn, to obtain technical training which may lead to well-paid, skilled work, so as to have their destinies in their own hands. They do not imagine that a vote will give them all they require, but they know it will supply them with a powerful lever to be used for their own advancement.

It cannot be supposed that the mere act of marking a paper and handing it to a returning officer, makes so remarkable a change in the character and attractions of women, as they already do this in thousands of cases in municipal and other local elections. It is, rather, that this parliamentary vote, which has undoubtedly become the hall-mark of citizenship in the British Isles, would, if bestowed on women, be the recognition of an altered state of things—the public admission of women to a position of equality. But if this change has already to a great extent taken place, there is something childish about refusing the hall-mark to what nevertheless is genuine metal, and there is certainly an injustice in a departure from rules that apply to all other citizens.

Women do not themselves believe that they are making themselves a whit less "womanly," taking the word in its most worthy and least frivolous sense, by claiming a vote; on the contrary, they are striving to place their own sex in a higher and worthier position, honestly believing that by so doing they are working for the benefit of the men as well as of the women.

They are often told that they will have to give up all the little attentions and civilities that are so dear to them, if they claim equal rights before the law. But even were this the case, how many women would this touch? How much politeness and attention would the toiling working woman have to sacrifice? But her more gently nurtured sister need have no fear. Men will continue to court favour with pretty faces, and do homage to the queens of society, be there votes or be there none; and it would indeed require the darkest of pessimists to declare that the world will deteriorate so much, that if women have votes all true chivalry will vanish, that chivalry which helps the weak and supports the feeble, which pays no attention to youth, or looks, or wealth, but gives help in time of need.

If we come to think of it, the amount of civility and attention now paid by men to women in society is not so very extensive. If men wait on women in public, do not women always wait on men in private? And they will certainly continue to cook the dinners, and warm the slippers, and lay the newspaper, all cut and folded, at the man's elbow, even should they afterwards find time to read that newspaper themselves.

Careful politicians always seriously consider the consequences of their acts before making any important change in the machinery of government; but were undue weight to be assigned to all the imaginary and illusory consequences which can be conjured up, there would never be any changes at all! And women resent the idea of being made to pay even the conventionalities and politenesses of an artificial society in exchange for their rights. They do not consider that the present suppositious contract is advantageous for them. The old feudal law of Europe broke down principally because, though the vassals performed their part of the contract, by supplying soldiers and service to their feudal chiefs, they did not in return get that protection and help they were entitled to expect. Even where this assistance was granted, the bargain was found to be unfair and too onerous on the vassals. So women, however grateful for protection and help, find that in an enormous number of cases they have to do without it, and that even where they obtain it, too much is expected in return; so that, like the feudal vassals, they have in the long run the worst of the bargain. They consider that, if it is once proved that for the general benefit they should be enfranchised, the liberty should be granted them without any attempt at barter.

The popular phrase, "A woman's sphere," is supposed by many to have a most potent effect in withstanding any claims to enfranchisement. Yet there are such differences of opinion as to what is a man's sphere, or what is a woman's sphere, that they might at least be left to settle for themselves what each can do best. A century ago, to wield the needle would have at least been conceded to women; and yet men have so far intruded themselves on women's work, that most of the clothes of the men and part even of the clothes of the women are now "tailor-made."

Again, midwifery used to be entirely in the hands of women, and here also men have gradually absorbed the best-paying part of a feminine calling. Without for a moment claiming that men should give up these occupations, it does strike one as a little hard that women should so often be reproached for not remaining in their own sphere.[1]

The effect on women generally of treating them as responsible persons cannot but be beneficial in the long run. It has been remarked that of all religious communities, that one which has treated women with the greatest respect, and placed them in a position of both equality and responsibility, is the Society of Friends. And Quaker women are admitted by all to have been worthy of the confidence bestowed on them, and to have less of that frivolity and irresponsibility with which women are so constantly reproached, and which has repeatedly been put forward as an argument for preventing their acquiring electoral rights.

When the Irish Church was disestablished by Mr. Gladstone's first administration in 1869, a great opportunity was lost of enlisting women's devotion and enthusiasm. The Irish Episcopal Church had to be reorganized on an independent footing, and it was proposed by the more advanced and enlightened section of the clergy to give the female members of the congregation some such acknowledged position as the women already enjoyed in the Presbyterian communities. The suggestion, though approved by many, was perhaps before its time, and fell to the ground ; but now, when there has been sufficient time to realize the numerical inferiority of Protestants in Ireland, regrets are constantly heard that a more liberal course was not adopted.

[1] See Appendix IV.

It is hoped, too, that by giving women votes, it will save many, especially in the more well-to-do classes, from the *ennui* and absence of interest from which large numbers suffer. It is of course possible to take an interest in public affairs without possessing a vote; but its possession undoubtedly has an astonishing effect in creating a general steady interest in politics at all times, that is so much more beneficial and desirable, than the feverish and short-lived excitement that bursts out in moments of panic. To have a vote is to wait for the election day rather than to rush into a revolution, and though women alone are hardly likely to disturb the public peace, yet it must be remembered that revolutions are brought about by those who have no votes, and who despair of other methods of reform, and that there has never yet been a revolution in which women have not played an important part.

Votes mean responsibility, and though men can never prevent women from interesting themselves in politics, they run all the danger of leaving power in the hands of irresponsible persons. And here we touch on another favourite argument of the enemy. Women, they say, have already so much power; it is unfair to increase it by giving them votes as well. But surely we may reply, that it is rather an exchange of power than an increase that is claimed.

Women have always exercised a certain sort of political power. Whether in ancient or modern history, we see women wielding power, sometimes for good, but in an enormous number of cases merely with a view to self-interest and intrigue. Every court is the scene of back-stairs influence, of favouritism, at times of gross venality, carried on to a great extent by women. At first sight this hardly encourages men to add to the power of women; but, on going further into the question, it soon appears that all this influence is irresponsible, that it cannot be called to account, that it is exercised by those women who have least want of it, and who are not suffering as much as many of their sisters from injustice and hard laws.

It is degrading and injurious to women, however pleasant it may be to the vanity of men, that to get an injustice put right, or a grievance attended to, they should always have to cajole and wheedle, to scheme and plot. And while the less worthy of their sisters are thus employed, the dumb thousands of the working women have no means of getting their wants attended to at all. There are good reasons for believing that should women be entrusted with direct and responsible power, it would counteract the evils of back-stairs influence, and to a great extent replace it altogether.

There is, too, it must not be forgotten, a more legitimate power wielded by a certain number of women. They have acquired it by their intellect, by their knowledge of human character, by that keen insight and quick intuition so characteristic of the superior feminine mind, that enables them to see their way clearly through the most tangled web of politics. But to increase power of this sort by means of a vote could surely do no harm.

CHAPTER III.

REPLY TO HABITUAL OBJECTIONS—EXPEDIENCY.

It is often assumed that women can stand quite aloof from politics, and it is urged that to give them votes would be to drag them into political life, to which otherwise they would be entire strangers. As a matter of fact the positions are exactly reversed. It is politics that come to women, that step into their every-day home life, that attract their interest in every direction the more educated they become.

The more social questions come to the front, the more impossible will it be to say that women have nothing to do with politics. No religious woman, of whatever creed, can fail to discover that, in a country where the Church and the State are connected, politics step into religious matters. No mother of a family can ignore the intrusion of politics into the questions of the education of her children, the vaccination of her babies, the sanitary condition of her home. No woman householder can imagine politics to be a closed book for her, when every war increases her income-tax, and constant Acts of Parlia-

Women strongly invaded c̄ church & cause involved c̄ the state + its politics

ADVANTAGES OF A VOTE.

ment affect her rates. Let men first invent a means of shutting off politics from women, before asking women to leave politics alone.

The arguments against Women's Suffrage, based on the probable use women would make of their votes, are less weighty. It is feared by some that they would join together and vote all one way, thereby upsetting the balance of parties. It is admitted as probable that, to abolish a certain number of grievances specially affecting women, there would be a tendency among them to unite in order to return candidates representing their views. But few will deny their right to do as much as this.

On general politics it seems as unlikely that women will all vote alike, as that men should suddenly all agree to vote against them. Men are influenced in the sides they take by their temperaments, by their education and bringing up, by their surroundings, by the books they read, by their interests and occupations; and why women should be supposed to be free from all these influences it is difficult to say.

If we were to adopt universal suffrage in England undoubtedly the fact that women predominate in numbers would increase the fears of those who dread to be ruled by them; but the question at present is a much narrower one, as in any case the women householders could never outvote the men. And, again, it must be remembered that, under the ballot, it would be impossible to ascertain whether the women had voted together or not.

Far from any danger of their solidarity, those who

have tried to improve the position of working women, have always complained of their want of cohesion. At present they seem, whether from defective education or other reasons, to have distinctly less tendency to co-operate than men, so that the fear of their all voting together appears to be purely illusory.

As long as they are deprived of political rights, there is certainly some danger of their ideas being out of harmony with those of men. It is constantly observed by English people that immense difficulties, and even dangers, arise in France from the fact that the women there are brought up with totally different ideas and habits and religion to the men. But these difficulties have never yet arisen in England, and are never likely to arise, if the political progress of the men is accompanied by a like advancement in the other sex. It is only when we see men making rapid strides towards complete enfranchisement, that we begin to discern a gulf between the two sexes which might tend to throw them each into opposing camps; but allow women to advance side by side with men, and all danger of their voting "solid" vanishes directly.

With regard to the political party women would be most inclined to join, there are singularly opposing views. It is contended by many that women are naturally conservative. It is urged that their love of order, their habits of obedience, the narrowness of the grooves in which they move, their dislike to changes causing disorder or disturbance, their love of property and possession, would all tend to make them vote for Conservatives.

But it is as often put forward that they are imaginative, that they are easily carried away by novel ideas and chimeras, that in foreign countries they have befriended Nihilists and Communists and revolutionaries of the most dangerous descriptions, that the majority of the women now agitating for votes hold advanced views and would influence other women in the use of their votes, and that, in fact, not only the Liberal party, but the extreme Radical party, could count on an increase of its voting power.[1]

But it is useless to discuss on which side women would vote, as, whatever the answer, it should not for a moment influence any honest politician in deciding whether to grant Women's Suffrage. Every extension of the franchise is a leap in the dark as to the results, and it is well it should be, for it is certainly most undesirable that it should be granted as a reward to people for holding certain political opinions. It has already been pointed out, and must not be forgotten, that even when women had voted, it would be impossible, on account of the ballot, to obtain any accurate statistics showing on which side they had bestowed their favours.

There is a great and genuine fear in the minds of many men that a woman would not vote according to her own judgment, but would take the advice of the clergyman, or priest, or minister of the church to which she might happen to belong, and thus practically put her vote into his pocket. An Englishman is especially likely to fear

[1] See Appendix V.

this, as, apart from the question of whether he is himself of a religious temperament or not, he has always had a strong dislike to any priestly interference in secular matters, and more particularly in politics; and Englishmen generally describe those who think otherwise as priest-ridden.

It is generally admitted that the tendency of education is to make both men and women more inclined to trust to their own judgment and to lean less blindly on others. The present rapid growth of female education ought therefore before long to supersede this difficulty altogether. Women have certainly shown themselves in the past less "priest-ridden" in England than in many other countries, and the absence of convents has placed the education of girls almost more in secular hands than that of boys.

Even if English women to a certain extent take the advice of their spiritual pastors in political matters, they will only follow the example of many men in so doing; neither will the consequences be as injurious as if, like a certain number of male electors, they were to vote merely from self-interest. The influence of the priest is at least as respectable as the influence of the publican, and it is quite certain that women will be less governed by the beer-interest than men.

But supposing every woman's vote were in the pocket of a priest, the political result in England would not be so very formidable. The Nonconformist ministers, who, not being State servants, feel much more at liberty to take an active part in elections than the Church of

England clergy, would almost invariably incline to the Liberal party, while the latter would put in a word for the Conservatives; consequently, the result, as far as can be judged, would be a probable equipoise. But putting aside the question of the party that would benefit most from the interference of the clergy, it must be remembered that here again a test is imposed on women, and not on men, and it is a religious test, moreover, which is somehow peculiarly repugnant to modern ideas.

Some say that women do not want votes, and that if they had them they would not make use of them. This argument was constantly used during the American Civil War about the slaves. It was said that the slaves did not want to be free, were much happier in bondage, and would not know what to do with themselves, or how to earn a livelihood if emancipated. It is true, that although the right to vote at parliamentary elections certainly existed for women before the Reform Bill of 1832,[1] and had in former times occasionally been exercised, yet it had fallen entirely into disuse, and no woman had voted for half a century, so that their exclusion from that Bill was at least excusable. But in view of the steady increase of feminine interest in political matters, it is at least certain that even after the first curiosity and novelty of having a vote had passed away, a considerable proportion of women would continue to go to the poll.

The only reliable statistics we can go upon are those

[1] See Appendix VI.

of the municipal elections, in which women have for some time taken part, and they certainly have done so in sufficient numbers to refute any allegations of indifference.

But even with regard to the voting at municipal elections, the statistics are very limited, as the passing of the Ballot Act made all official returns of the kind impossible, and we can only refer to those few years between the admission of women to the municipal franchise and the passing of the Ballot Act. Yet in 1870, 25 per cent. of the women on the register voted, although the novelty of polling had disappeared; and the proportion of men who voted is only slightly greater. This was fifteen years ago, and there is every reason to believe, though it cannot be demonstrated by figures, that women take an increased interest in public affairs now, and that a larger proportion take part in municipal elections now than they did at that time. It is well known that among men the proportion who vote at a General Election is much larger than at any local contest, and so it undoubtedly would be with women. An interesting point to be observed about these elections for Town Councils is that the proportions rise and fall together, showing that what interests the male section of the community has precisely the same effect on the female section.

If people wish for a thing, they not only ask for it themselves, but work for it and make sacrifices to obtain it. The agitation for Women's Suffrage has been supported by thousands of women at meetings; they have signed their names to petitions in enormous numbers, and have given money and time and trouble and thought to the agitation ; so that the argument that women do not want the vote does not at any rate apply to them. Whether a plebiscite of the women of the British Isles would accept or reject the franchise, there is no means of telling; but those who do demand it, wish to point out that in any case voting is never compulsory, and that no woman would be forced to vote unless she wished.

Were votes given to the women householders from motives of justice and expediency, and they all, save one, declined or neglected to exercise their right, that one should not be deprived of her vote because of the others. As we know, moreover, that at any rate a certain number of women would value the vote, for they are undoubtedly making sacrifices to obtain it, there is no need to ask what the other women would do.

Women would not be dragged unwillingly into the whirlpool of politics any more than the men who now prefer to stand aloof. They would at long intervals, once or twice in five or six years, receive the visits of the political canvassers, who would certainly not waste their time in trying to force the doors of those who preferred to keep them shut.

The idea that elections and political meetings are necessarily scenes of disorder and strife belongs to a previous state of existence. With the secrecy of the ballot, the admission of the large masses of the people to the franchise, and the stringent regulations of the Corrupt Practices Act, the tendency is every year greater to have orderly and quiet elections even when party feeling runs high.

Had women to go to the poll it would tend to order and quiet to a yet greater extent. The well-known example of the Territory of Wyoming, in the United States, cannot be too often quoted, as there the franchise was given to the women with the stated object of seeing whether it would not put an end to the turbulence and violence that had so long disgraced the district. And the success was complete. If the men all knew that their female relatives must pass through the streets on the election day, they would have the greatest inducement to assist in the preservation of order.

It is too late to protest against the appearance of women on public platforms, or against their taking part in the proceedings, for that has become so frequent as no longer to excite the astonishment or shock the feelings of any audience. As a matter of fact, it is probable, that were Women's Suffrage passed, there would be less occasion for them to appear in public than there is now, though undoubtedly they would continue to do so, as occasion might arise.

Most of the women now engaged in agitating this question wish to avoid any unnecessary show of hostility towards men. They feel deeply a sense of injustice, or, as Mr. Gladstone once put it, "that women obtain less than justice;"[1] but they think a change of the law will be better promoted if they point out in a straightforward manner their grievances and their wrongs, rather than if they attack the motives and proceedings of the men who made that law. Men certainly complain if any hostility is shown towards them, and are apparently aggrieved if any acrimony is allowed to appear, even when unredressed grievances are under discussion; but those who believe that it is impossible for men really to know what women want and feel unless they have women as constituents, do well not to attack them too bitterly for their inevitable mistakes.

Some men seem to think that women would like to have all the advantages, and none of the disadvantages of the position of citizens. But when and where have women advocated anything but equality? The Married Women's Property Act of 1882 not only secured a woman in the enjoyment of her own property, but threw upon her many liabilities as well, which she had hitherto escaped. It enabled her to be either a trustee or a bankrupt, and it made her property liable for the maintenance of the family; but women gladly accepted these new duties and liabilities as the logical outcome of their new position.

The most is made of one or two small inequalities of the law, which are rather the effect of careless legislation than any deliberate intention of benefiting women to the

[1] See Appendix VII.

exclusion of men. At present a magistrate may grant a judicial separation to a wife who has been beaten or severely ill-used by her husband, while in the rare cases of a husband suffering from his wife's assaults, he is unable to obtain this relief. But women would be the first to place this law on an equal footing, if men required their assistance in order to do so.

It is sometimes urged that women are not a separate class, and that therefore they do not need any separate votes or voice in the government. But the only possible meaning of the expression, "a separate class," is a number of people for whom different rules and regulations are required from their neighbours. Do away with the present political disabilities of women, and they will to that extent cease to be a class. But political power is not now given to one class and withheld from another. The tendency of the age is to endeavour to obliterate class distinctions, and it is as individuals rather than as a class that women claim the right to vote.

It is constantly assumed that every woman has a husband, or a father, or a brother, capable and willing to fight for her interests as well as his own, and defend her in all troubles, and advise her in all difficulties. But unfortunately there exists an immense number of women who are not shut up in glass cases in this way, who have no near relatives to whom they have the right to apply for help on all occasions, and who from one cause or another, and generally from circumstances not under their own control, are entirely dependent on their own resources; and the fact that in all legislation their position and very existence is entirely left out of account, does not tend to lessen their troubles, or make the earning of daily bread less toilsome and difficult.

CHAPTER IV.

THE HARDSHIPS OF EXCLUSION.

EVERY argument that has been used during the last half-century for the enfranchisement of the working classes, whether in the towns or in the counties, applies with equal force to women; and it is curious to hear these arguments constantly used by those who refuse to carry them to their logical conclusion.[1]

It has been said, a vote is a great educator; give a man a vote, even be he ignorant and illiterate, and the first use he will make of it will be to get for his children that very education in which he feels himself so deficient. Undoubtedly the progress of national education has gone hand in hand with the enfranchisement of the people, though it is somewhat difficult to prove which is cause and which is effect. Education is probably in its most backward stages among the agricultural labourers who benefit by the recent Reform Bill, and it will be interesting to note whether they will not rise both in intelligence and education to the level of their brother

[1] See Appendix VIII.

workmen in the towns, now that politically they are on an equal footing. But while among the men, education and enfranchisement thus march hand in hand and help each other forward, women have the harder task of educating themselves first, in order to show that they are fit for the franchise.

The agricultural labourer is told that he is too submissive and too dependent, that he is ruled by the squire and the parson, and cannot even make advantageous terms with the farmer. He is told that if he is given a vote he will be able to change all this for himself; he will be able more easily to emigrate, or to combine with his fellows to obtain better terms at home, and generally to learn to think and act for himself, and to increase his self-respect and independence. This is a dangerous lesson to repeat in the ears of women if they are not to profit by it and apply it to their own position. They too are aiming at more independence and less artificial restraint; they too wish to combine to improve their wages and think for themselves. And to hear a vote held out as a means to all these desirable ends, tempts women to hasten towards the same goal.

Many of the farm labourers, by dint of care and self-sacrifice and years of thrift and temperance, have raised themselves to a position in which a vote was to be got even under the old restricted franchise. But a woman may be as thrifty and temperate, hard-working and careful as she likes—the vote still hangs out of her reach in the most tantalizing manner.

It has often been remarked that the law classes women with infants, criminals, and lunatics; but even in that doubtful company she holds an inferior position. A minor grows to manhood before many years are passed, a criminal resumes the rights of citizenship as soon as his sentence has elapsed, a lunatic may recover and vote as before; but a woman, do what she will, is always excluded. A fortune may be left her; she may attain celebrity in literature, art, or science; she may be upheld as a model of all the virtues; she may devote herself to her country, and pour out her wealth for its benefit—but a vote she has never any hope of reaching.

How often have the agricultural labourers been told that they are to be given votes because no one can tell their wants so well as themselves? But they are not only given power to legislate for themselves; they are to help to decide what is good for women as well, from the peeress in her own castle to the factory girl at her loom.

It must not be imagined that if nothing is done in the direction of giving voting power to women, that things will go on as they were before; that as women have managed to exist very fairly comfortably without votes hitherto, no very great harm will be done by letting things alone. Unfortunately for this comfortable and *fainéant* argument, if everything else improves and moves on, women alone will stand still and find themselves in the extremely inconvenient position of being left stranded with the tide of human progress flowing far away in another channel.

Their position will be very different and very much worse than in former times. Then, most men had no votes. Now, women alone will stand in the ranks of the governed, with all the men to govern them. For men will not consent to stand still, though the hopes of women remain stranded. Men are pushing on to manhood suffrage, while women, having failed to gain attention from the limited number of male-voters, have now to set about the task of converting the newly enfranchised millions. There was some sort of equality between men and women under the Georges, while under Queen Victoria women are forced to stand aside and let the men alone receive the badge of freedom.

The change caused by the ever-increasing population of the British Isles makes the position of the unenfranchised harder to bear. In a thinly peopled country personal liberty has full scope, and the government inspector is unknown. But in the crowded state of Britain to-day, existence is only possible under a system of elaborate inspection and regulation that threatens soon to outshine the most paternally governed continental State. Compulsory education, compulsory sanitary inspection, compulsory vaccination are all voted for by men who are willing to submit to them, and to pay for them. But women, with whom this army of inspectors and government officials interfere, perhaps more than with men, have to pay and submit without effectual means of expressing an opinion on the subject. To give up personal liberty of your own free will, for the benefit of your fellow-men, may be a duty; but to have it forced upon you by the votes of others is hardly distinguishable from tyranny.

Women fully realize the importance of obtaining suitable machinery before setting to work to improve their position, and it is for this reason that so many have concentrated their efforts on the attempt to obtain votes. Yet, were Parliament to put aside purely political questions, whether relating to its own constitution or to foreign affairs, and were to turn its attention to the social welfare of the people, it would be perceived at once how great a loss is the absence of women's opinion in arriving at a just conclusion. It is even to a certain extent recognized that here is women's sphere, and it is quite possible that the slow progress made in social reform, is due to the absence of women from political life, and a certain reluctance to plunge into it without their guidance. Land questions, as well as county government, have been postponed to see what the new voters under the Reform Bill have to say; and undoubtedly to attack social questions, with half the nation dumb, might seriously compromise the success of any such undertaking.

In the wide field of practical philanthropy there is room and work for both men and women, but undoubtedly there is a great deal that is best done by the voluntary help of sensible women. And there are an enormous number in the field. Whether their work consist of rent-collecting, of befriending young girls and finding them employment, of nursing the sick poor in their own homes, of distributing charity to the deserving, of rescuing women from the ranks of vice, the number who have gained experience and knowledge that would be of help in coping with poverty and crime is every day increasing. Nor are the religious bodies behindhand in getting women to penetrate even the worst slums of the metropolis. The Bible women and the mission women know more of the darker sides of life than the great body of ordinary electors; and they would be less likely to vote for make-shift remedies had they the power.

Besides, Acts of Parliament alone will not make a people moral and cleanly and sober, though they may go far to encourage these qualities. Show women that they too are interested in the welfare of the nation by entrusting them with votes, and they will be the first to give that personal work, to advise, to comfort, and to teach, without which Acts of Parliament on social questions are apt to become so much waste paper.

To women's honour, be it said, they have already done much in this direction, but to withhold what many consider their right is hardly the way to encourage them to walk in the paths of disinterested citizenship. It is only those who have attempted to grapple with the difficult problems of social and moral regeneration, who realize how dangerous it is to leave any power for good slumbering unused, while all the evil influences have full swing. We cannot afford to do it. Women have leisure, women have sensitive feelings and acute perceptions; they could make use of their knowledge, and prevent disastrous legislative mistakes, had men some means of getting at their collective opinions. But as long as men prefer to trust entirely to themselves, improvement in certain directions is impeded if not altogether at a stand-still.

The political history of England may well be compared to the ebb and flow of the tide. First come periods of political excitement and reform, when progress, or at any rate change, makes rapid strides forward; and the time when there shall no longer exist any abuse to sweep away, seems rapidly approaching. But the greater the movement forward, the more certainly comes the reflux, when nothing is so much desired by the nation as to rest and be thankful, and a period of political stagnation sets in.

It is those who have no votes who suffer most from these varying phases of public life. In times of excitement their voices are not heard, or, if heard, they are harshly told this is no time to listen to small grievances. When quieter times set in, they are again thrust aside as ill-advised in proposing changes when all are yearning for peace. The consequence is that at one moment unjust laws slip through without the possibility of women procuring their rejection, or at least fair discussion; and at another no legislation at all can be obtained.

During the celebrated Midlothian campaign of 1879, Mr. Gladstone appealed to the women of Scotland for their help and influence.[1] But, to borrow a comparison recently used by Professor Stuart, M.P., it is no use asking women to pull a bell-rope when there is no bell attached to the other end.

If women had possessed votes during former administrations, undoubtedly the C. D. Acts would not have been imposed without a struggle, and the Factory Acts would have been submitted to a more thorough and impartial criticism, which would have caused the omission of several important clauses. The woman's task is indeed hard and discouraging when all her efforts fail to prevent the imposition of fresh disabilities, and when she herself so clearly sees what is wanted to prevent the forging of new chains.

In looking through the list of changes in the law that are now contemplated, it is possible to point out more than one instance of fresh disabilities likely to be imposed

---

[1] "I therefore think in appealing to you ungrudgingly to open your own feelings and play your own part in this political crisis we are making no inappropriate demand, but are beseeching you to fulfil the duties which belong to you, which, so far from involving any departure from your character as women, are associated with the fulfilment of that character and the performance of that duty, and the neglect of which would in future times be to you a source of pain and mortification, and the accomplishment of which would serve to gild your own future years with sweet remembrances, and to warrant you in hoping that each in your own place and sphere has raised your voice for justice and has striven to mitigate the sorrows and misfortunes of mankind."

on women, unless they are first given that useful defensive weapon called a vote. Will men deny that the question of " Marriage with a Deceased Wife's Sister " is of importance to women? Some politicians, whose brains are not distinguished for lucidity, have a vague idea that they will for once be legislating for women by passing this Bill into law. Yet apart from the question of whether it is for the advantage of the family (and all second marriages must be examined from this point of view), and whether women are for or against it, undoubtedly it would create a fresh grievance and a new disability. If a widower is to be allowed to marry the sister of his late wife, so as to give his children a mother interested in them, why should not a widow be allowed to marry her deceased husband's brother if she consider it for the advantage of her young family? Many persons have a vague idea that one includes the other; others again are positive that the first is a most desirable arrangement, while words are not strong enough to denounce those who think the second quite as harmless. Women at any rate are logical enough to see that this is not a question that can be settled properly, unless all who are concerned have a voice in discussing it. To create so great a disability at the present time, would give a fatal blow to the belief that men may be trusted to see justice done to women.

There is a strong inclination in the House of Commons to throw the expenses of the returning officer during elections on to the rates, instead of as at present making the candidates themselves pay. A Bill with this object was even read a second time in 1882. However much may be said for such a measure by those who are both ratepayers and voters, would not this also be a fresh grievance for women who would have to pay for elections in which they take no part?

This is exactly what takes place now wherever a constituency is suspected of corrupt practices. A commission is appointed to hold meetings and examine witnesses in the accused place, and the whole of the expenses of this commission, whether the verdict is ultimately "guilty" or "not guilty," are thrown on the ratepayers. Sometimes this fine amounts to as much as a shilling in the pound. The poor householders of the female sex are thus severely punished for a crime they have not even had a chance of committing, for no candidate or his agent would waste money in bribing a woman householder, while a male voter may possibly have received money from both sides.

The hardship arising from being a responsible householder, and yet being without a vote, is exemplified in a small way by the Registration of Voters Act 1885. Every householder is required, under a penalty of forty shillings, to make a return of every male person employed by him or her, for the purpose of registering all those, who, living under a separate roof, may, under the service franchise, be entitled to a vote. Thus a woman farmer has herself to cause to be registered all the labourers on her farm, and though, it is to be hoped, most women are not selfish enough to wish to deprive any men of the much-prized vote, yet they cannot but feel bitterly the fact that they are entirely excluded, and may even be severely fined for neglecting to enfranchise others. It really seems an ingenious manner of officially informing women of the inferior position they hold; and though not in itself of very great importance, may lead them to a better understanding of all that their exclusion involves.

CHAPTER V.

PARTY POLITICS.

THIS question of Women's Suffrage has hitherto been successfully prevented from falling into the hands of any party in the House of Commons, or indeed in the country. Whatever may be the arguments for party government, all questions that have not been made "Government questions" stand on firmer footing if they trust to the arguments that appeal to sensible persons, and accept support from whatever side it is offered.

Undoubtedly many of the advocates of Women's Suffrage have been known as strong partisans, but every division list shows support from Liberals and Conservatives, Whigs and Radicals, Home Rulers and Ulster members. The same disregard of party is apparent in the opposition to the measure, as members of all parties have voted against it. The speakers who have supported this reform in the House of Commons are drawn from all sides, and the tellers for Women's Suffrage in the last division (1884) were, as on former occasions, one a Liberal and the other a Conservative (Mr. Woodall and Baron de Worms).[1]

It has of late, for various reasons, become increasingly difficult for a private member successfully to pilot any Bill that rouses opposition through the House of Commons; the probability is therefore that, as the question cannot much longer remain unsettled, it will fall into the hands of either the Conservative or the

---

[1] The following analysis of the two last divisions may be found interesting as showing the division of parties. The tellers are included.

	IN FAVOUR.					AGAINST.			
	L.	C.	H.R.	TOTAL		L.	C.	H.R.	TOTAL
1883	84	19	13	116	1883	51	78	3	132
1884	32	96	9	137	1884	236	27	10	273

The following are the numbers of the divisions taken in the House of Commons on the question of Women's Suffrage. In some cases a Bill was submitted, at other times a resolution; and in the last case an amendment to a Bill already before the House, which accounts for the falling off of support and the increase of the majority against.

	IN FAVOUR.	AGAINST.
1867	75	196
1870		
Second Reading	124	91
Committee stage	94	220
1871	151	220
1872	143	222
1873	155	222
1875	152	187
1876	152	238
1878	140	219
1879	103	217
1883	114	130
1884	135	271

Liberal party and become a Government measure. But it would be impossible at present to say which party will distinguish itself by taking it up. When this event does occur it is, however, certain that a number of old friends from the opposite camp will continue to give the reform their faithful support.

In arguing the question at public debates, or speaking about it at public meetings, it is found a great advantage to be able to say with a clear conscience to any person inclined to be friendly, that this is a cause above party politics, and can safely be supported on its merits alone.

In looking at the past history of the movement, it is evident that it originated as a practical question among Liberals of an advanced type, such as Mr. John Stuart Mill and Mr. Jacob Bright, who are the best known among the supporters of the question when first raised in the House of Commons. It is also obvious that while the support on the Liberal side has been maintained, the present Parliament has seen a considerable increase of interest on the Conservative benches.

Those who believe in the innate conservatism of the female mind, and ground their opposition on this most problematical theory, are wont to declare that this increase of support is mainly due to selfish and interested considerations. But seeing that ample arguments exist for disinterested and reasonable Conservative support, women at any rate will be inclined to give them the benefit of the doubt.

It is surely a logical argument to advance, that since men no longer hold the franchise in trust for one another, they can no longer be supposed to hold it in trust for women.[1] Whereas formerly there was an attempt to place votes in the hands of a selected and superior class, that system has been found impracticable, all barriers have been swept away, and the franchise has been given as a right to the many rather than as a trust to the few. How, then, is it possible to exclude a body of persons, large numbers of whom are equal in education, intelligence, property, and conduct, to those who formerly were the selected electors of the country? By their inclusion the standard might have been kept level, but by shutting them out, the only possible additions have been from an inferior class of persons.

The upper classes in this country, among whom Conservatism naturally finds a majority of supporters, are able better to appreciate the bitter feelings of a woman who, if she be a landowner or the mistress of a fortune, sees every servant and dependent on her estate given a vote as soon as she has provided him with a separate dwelling, while she alone is excluded.

In former times she had much political influence and power. It was considered most fitting and proper that the mistress of many acres should direct the opinions and more or less dispose of the votes of all who lived on her land. Now, the ballot has made every vote secret, and "undue influence" is a heavily punished crime under the

[1] See Appendix IX.

[undue influence]

Corrupt Practices Acts. To these women Conservatives would only be restoring, in a more legitimate and beneficial form, the power of former times. Politicians, who fear the use to be made of political power by those who never have wielded it before, are anxious to counteract it by the enfranchisement of the women of the upper and middle classes, who they hope will be more amenable to the prejudices, beliefs, and sentiments of their own class.

These same persons would desire once and for all to close the reform question, so as to remain on the safe landing-stage of household suffrage. They foresee that if numbers of women agitate for enfranchisement, the whole question of Reform may again come up at any moment, and universal suffrage be hastened, when it is perceived that household suffrage is not even a reality.

Nothing would so much tend to close, at any rate for the present, the whole era of Parliamentary Reform, as the inclusion of *every householder*, male or female, within its bounds.

This is an opinion held not only by Conservatives anxious to vote for women householders, but by those advanced Radicals who are most eager for universal suffrage. They do not wish to close the whole question and make the present system so logical that it would be difficult to supersede. They would be ready even to vote against Women's Suffrage altogether, while approving of it, rather than postpone for a few years the manhood suffrage they are aiming at.

There are many, too, who are afraid of the admission

of women householders, as in their hearts they believe it would prove so excellent and just a measure, that a more extended claim would be based upon its evident success; but it will be best in a separate chapter to discuss to what extent women should at present be granted votes.

CHAPTER VI.

WOMEN'S GRIEVANCES.

It is necessary carefully to examine the grievances from which women suffer, and of which they constantly complain, as they have certainly been the primary cause of the claim for the franchise. And yet it would be a great mistake, by accentuating these grievances, <u>to let any men suppose, as some undoubtedly do already, that they have only to cure these legislative mistakes in order to put an end to the agitation.</u>

Were all the inequalities smoothed away, women, unless they had the vote, would never feel that they could prevent the same or other inequalities from being reestablished. Besides, women would then be admittedly on an equality with men, and it would be difficult to say why, if not inferior beings, they should be deprived of any rights that men possessed.

To return to the well-worn comparison between the condition of women and that of slaves, it would hardly be contended that, even were all slaves well treated by their owners, slavery would be an excellent institution, and worthy to be upheld. Before the abolition of slavery this argument was constantly used, and yet, from its inherent viciousness, slavery had died out in many countries where slaves were usually well cared for. And now, that the cruelty practised in particular cases on slaves is no longer prominently before the public, the whole institution is none the less condemned as mischievous in its immediate results and disastrous in its after consequences. The cruel treatment merely appealed more vividly to the imaginations of the people, and brought home to them, as no arguments could ever do, the iniquity of the system.

And so it is with women's grievances. They have caused the whole question of women's position and rights to be discussed and canvassed, and every act of injustice that entails misery on some woman is turned to good account as an argument for the improvement of her condition before the law. But were every law that bears heavily on women repealed, the injustice of their exclusion from the polling-booth would still remain the same, and the agitation for votes would continue as before, their claim resting on a solid footing of reason and common sense rather than on any grievance, however hard to bear.

At the same time, were even a small section of women allowed votes, their first energies would be directed towards the repeal of unequal laws, and all who are now labouring in that direction would find their task materially facilitated.

The grievances may be divided under seven headings :

I. Custody and guardianship of children.
II. Divorce and marriage laws.
III. Protection of the person.
IV. Property laws.
V. Testamentary laws.
VI. Taxation.
VII. Trade regulations.

The rights of parents over their children are certainly very simple, if not very just. One parent, the father, has all the rights, the other, the mother, has none. It says much for the forbearance of the average Englishman, that with so unlimited a power in his hands, he has, on the whole, so little abused it. Had there been more frequent cases of the enforcement of the father's rights, at the expense of an innocent mother, it is hardly possible to believe that the present state of the law could have continued untouched up to this day. For once men appear to have realized that though

> " It is excellent
> To have a giant's strength, . . . it is tyrannous
> To use it like a giant."

In every other civilized country, and in many that are usually held to be outside the pale of civilization, the mother has legally some claim, some rights over her own offspring; in England her rights cannot be said to exist. "The father alone has the power to direct their education, to decide in what religion they are to be instructed, to apprentice them to any trade without the mother's consent, and to take their earnings. He can say where and with whom they shall reside, and can not only take them from their mother whilst they are infants, but can send them to a foreign country if he think fit. In no case has the mother any remedy unless she is rich enough to invoke the aid of the Court of Chancery, and then the court will help her only if she can prove—(*a*) That the children have suffered serious physical and moral injury from the treatment of the father. (*b*) That the conduct of the father has been such as to entitle her to a separation. But though the law gives all the power to the father alone, the mother is bound by law to maintain the children out of her own earnings, if from any cause the father fails to do so. She cannot compel him to support the children; he may refuse, and it is not until she goes into the workhouse that the Poor Law Guardians interfere, and make him pay for the maintenance of his family through an order obtained from a magistrate. If he refuse this order he can be sent to prison, but in no case is he obliged to give more than a pauper's allowance for them."[1]

It is not only during the lifetime of the father that the custody of the children is entirely left to him; after his death he has still more power over them than the living mother. He may by will appoint any person guardian without even consulting his wife, and this guardian exercises all control over the home, the religion, and the educa-

[1] See "What is women's suffrage, and why do women want it?" by "Veritas."

tion of the children. And if a man die intestate, or if he omit in his will to appoint guardians for his children, the mother does not even then necessarily become the legal guardian. The husband's male relatives may come forward as his representatives, and claim the guardianship of the children. The woman has no similar rights in case of her death; she cannot appoint a guardian to fill her place in case her husband marry again or neglect her children; she cannot even appoint a guardian when her husband is already dead, and she is likely to follow him to the grave.

Women must remember that no promise made by a man before marriage, even should the marriage be conditional on that promise, can deprive him of these rights. He may break every promise with regard to his children, and the law will sanction his conduct.[1]

It is not until the year 1884 that we find any attempt was made to legislate in this matter. Mr. Bryce was indeed able in that session to carry a Bill through the House of Commons altering the present state of the law. But while it was at first drawn with a view to give women equality with their husbands in all matters relating to their children, in its course through committee it was so mutilated and restricted as to be comparatively valueless. The consequence was that when the House of Lords quietly suspended it for future consideration, its best friends hardly thought it worth while to enter a protest. No further legislative progress has been made since that

[1] See Appendix X.

time, in spite of some futile attempts to obtain a discussion during the late session of 1885.

It appeared from the debates on this Bill that although many Members of Parliament admit that a woman has the first claim over her children after her husband's death, comparatively few think that she should have equal rights over them during his lifetime. Under the circumstances, it seems unlikely that any drastic change in the law is probable.

It is extraordinary to find how much ignorance exists in England both among fathers and mothers on the point of their respective rights over the children, and it is only when they disagree that they realize the position. But it is a question upon which there is much greater unanimity among women than on any other point of the women's rights platform, as few women with children of their own can fail to believe in their moral rights over them.

From the question of the custody of children, it is natural to pass at once to the inequalities in the marriage and divorce law, as it is impossible to consider the justice of equal rights to divorce without finding the question of the custody of children continually cropping up.

The present divorce law dates from 1857, that is to say, a few years before women seriously combined to ask for votes. As is well known, the divorce law requires a woman to prove two conjugal crimes against her husband before she is given a divorce, while he has only to convict her of one; thereby setting up a separate code of morality for each sex.

This inability of a woman to obtain a divorce, except in very gross cases, combined with the absence of rights over her children, place her most unfairly in the power of her husband. It must, and does constantly occur, that where a wife is treated with brutal violence by her husband, she cannot leave him even to return to her own parents or friends, as she would then be obliged to leave her children in his custody, to bear all the brunt of his ill-will against her. The more tenderly does she perform her maternal duties, the more impossible is it for her to escape from the tyranny of a man whose crimes against her fall short of the required number for a divorce.

It must not be forgotten that the consequences to a woman of having her home broken up, and herself turned out into the streets, are always much more severe than on a man; and would always prevent a certain number of women from appealing to the divorce courts even had they the same facilities as men; so that to increase the difficulties of appeal seems doubly unjust.

It would almost appear, from the severity with which women are treated with regard to their children, that they more commonly neglect their duties towards them; and yet it is notorious that the number of cases where they are deserted by the father is immensely greater than where the mother abandons them. It is generally considered that the loss to at any rate small children of a mother, is greater than the loss of a father, so that unfair legislation tending to the banishment of the mother, not only weighs on women, but injuriously affects their children. In every way the present English divorce law controverts the maxim that the law is intended for the protection of the weak.

The idea that <u>marriage is a state of subjection rather than equality,</u> is perhaps fostered by the different vows that the Church of England Marriage Service contains. But as men notoriously do not take seriously the words, "With all my worldly goods I thee endow," so it is possible they do not take literally the promise of the bride to "obey." It is but fair to remark that the civil contract does not contain any inequalities.

 The third complaint, with regard to <u>the protection given by law to the persons of women,</u> has already in one phase been touched on in the previous paragraph. It has for long been observed as a tendency of English law, and as the practice of English magistrates and juries, to view with much greater leniency any crime against the person than any attack on property.

When it is considered that the House of Commons, the bench, and the jury-box are entirely filled with men, it cannot be wondered at. Men, as a rule, can defend their own persons against any ordinary attack, but call in the help of the law to defend property which they hold in such large quantities as to make it impossible for the owners to defend it personally. Women, on the other hand, have comparatively little or no property to defend, but are incapable of effectually defending their own persons.

It is curious to note that the law defends a man's property, even against his own folly, until he is twenty-one years of age. But a girl's virtue, which is too often her sole possession, was up to this year (1885) only defended by the law till she was fourteen. That, by the Criminal Law Amendment Act, the age should have been raised to sixteen is a manifest improvement. A man may commit gross acts of violence against a woman, and only be condemned to pay a fine; but if he be hungry and steal a loaf, or ragged and steal a pair of boots, all the majesty of the law rises up to punish such an outrage on property, and he is probably thrown into prison.

As long as the laws that regulate the relations between the sexes are on so unequal a footing, it is useless to hope that public opinion will do much to alter this state of affairs. And on this question, at least, as much must be effected by public opinion acting on magistrates and juries as by any legislative change.

The high importance attached by men to property is apparent in the fact that they have shown themselves much quicker and more eager to remedy the injustice of the law of married women's property, than any other grievance. Successive acts have been passed with the object, firstly, of securing to a woman the wages she has earned by her own toil or talent; and secondly, of allowing her to hold for her own separate use and benefit any money that may be left her by will.

The Married Women's Property Act of 1883 has been found a just and equable arrangement which has already conferred far-reaching benefits, and, having been passed with the help and good-will of many of the most able lawyers of the country, it is hoped that the principle it maintains of equal rights will serve as an excellent precedent in other matters.

But it leaves untouched the laws of primogeniture and entail which bear particularly hardly upon women; and although the number of entailed estates is not so very great in England, the existence of such an arrangement fosters the idea that women are of an inferior order, and incapable of managing a large landed property. In scores of families, that are never likely to own any land at all, the education and prospects of the girls are entirely subordinated to those of the boys; while in France, where entails and the rights of primogeniture were done away with during the first revolution, the equality of the law has brought about a corresponding fairness in public opinion, and girls are much more equally treated.

But it is unnecessary to insist much on this grievance, as at most it touches but a limited number of women, and rich women have always, to a certain extent, been considered by custom and by law. It is much more important that poor women should be confirmed in the possession of their earnings, and be able to keep a separate account in their own names at the savings bank, and this at any rate is now the law.

The history of the passing of the Married Women's

Property Act is worth mentioning as a curious study for the parliamentary student, from the number of times it was rejected, or talked out, or counted out, or shunted, to allow some measure of more importance to men to be passed. But the steady persistence of a determined body of men and women was at last rewarded in 1882 by success, and the Act came into force January 1, 1883.

As regards the Intestacy Laws and the injustices arising from them, it will be best to quote a lawyer learned in the question. "One of the most notorious cases of inequality between the sexes, and that in a matter where there can be no reasonable excuse for it, is in the law of intestacy. Leaving out the law of the land, which does not affect women so often, and is not so unjust to them, let us see how the personal property of an intestate is distributed. A man dies intestate; one third of his property goes to his wife, and the rest to his children; or if he has no children, one half of it goes to his wife, and one half of it to his other relations. But if a woman dies intestate the *whole of her property* goes to her husband. Her children get nothing, and in case she has no children, her other relations get nothing either. Now observe the effect. Suppose a woman marries twice and dies without making a will, her children by her first husband are dependent on their stepfather's generosity. All their mother's fortune belongs to him. He can leave them their share of it if he likes; but if they quarrel with him he need not leave them a penny. The way in which a man's property goes upon his death without a will is fair enough, and should not the woman's be divided in the same way? And have not women a right to be consulted as to how their property should be distributed? In the same way women are unfairly treated in the distribution of an intestate's property where he, or she, dies unmarried. If a single man or a single woman die leaving a father or mother living, the *father* gets all the money and the mother nothing. If the intestate have a father, brothers, or sisters living, but no mother, the *father still takes all*. But if he leave no father, but mother, brothers, and sisters, the mother only takes a share with the brothers and sisters. By applying the simple principle that the sexes should be treated with absolute equality, all inconvenience might easily be remedied. Whatever the father has the mother ought to have the same. Whatever is the share of the husband, that should be the share of the wife. No assembly which had women amongst its constituents would think of upholding a system in which this equality was not observed."

The great grievance of taxation goes to the root of the whole question, and especially affects the unmarried women or widows who are heads of households. "Taxation without representation is tyranny," say the men in fine old constitutional language; but women have not yet got the saying applied to themselves. And on this point two courses are open to men. If they will not give women votes they might at least refuse to tax them.

Taxation without representation

Indeed the income-tax, when first collected, was not enforced on women's incomes; but now it is only the political canvasser that passes by a woman's door as he goes from house to house. The tax-gatherer and rate-collector call at every house, whoever it may be owned by; and the money may be spent with perfect impunity in ways highly obnoxious to women.

In a country where universal manhood suffrage is the law, the women have the same complaint to make, that the money they pay for the government of their country is spent without their control. But in England, where tax-paying and rate-paying is the basis of all enfranchisement, whether imperial or local, the injustice is much more flagrant.

It is property that is represented in the person of its owner, and Englishmen have shown great tenacity in keeping hold of the principle that votes are intended for the defence of property, and should only be in the hands of the owners of property. But women's property goes unrepresented and consequently undefended. It is quite a common saying that no person is so cheated and swindled out of property as a woman, but the unfortunate combination of no vote, and absence of education in business matters, is quite enough to account for this result.

. There are many excellent historical and constitutional precedents to justify those, who are taxed without their own consent and control, in refusing to pay. And a limited number of brave women have made use of this weapon, and allowed their goods to be seized and sold by public auction as a protest against such injustice. But for various reasons the example has not spread. Taxation is so complicated and far-reaching in modern times that no individual can exist long without contributing directly or indirectly to the service of the State.

Those who make use of this method suffer from the accusation that they set an example in breaking the law rather than in getting it altered, and though these reasons might in extreme cases be got over, yet as long as women have any hope of legislative redress, it is perhaps more judicious to refrain from so violent a remedy. The motives of those who have thus defied the tax-gatherer are certainly unexceptionable, and any action that draws attention to the whole question is probably indirectly useful, but on the whole the Women's Suffrage Society were probably judicious in refraining from taking any action in the matter.

Under the heading of "trade regulations" may be included the whole of the barriers, legal or professional, or merely customary, that make it difficult for women to earn a livelihood. These regulations have two evil consequences; in the first place, they seriously limit the number of employments open to women; in the second place, they beat down their wages very much beneath the amount ordinarily paid to men for the same work.[1]

Great efforts have been made by women of late years

[1] See Appendix XI.

to increase the number of employments open to workers of their own sex, but the rate at which women have crowded into the labour market has increased to a still greater extent. The disproportion between the sexes is undoubtedly one of the causes, and in a country where women preponderate by nearly a million, it is useless to suggest that marriage is their only calling.

The absence of training and technical education is another cause of low wages to many, but nothing affects so much the low rate of wages and the overcrowding of applicants for employment, as the regulations that prevent women from following more than a few occupations. The Factory Acts, by limiting the hours during which women may be employed to the day-time, shut them out from book-binding, printing, confectionery, and many other callings. And in numerous other cases, where in ordinary times they get excellent employment, the smallest press of business leading to overtime causes them to be dismissed and replaced by men.

Trades Unionism, too, tells heavily against them—often involuntarily, but sometimes by special regulations. Those lucrative and close trades unions, the Bar and the medical profession, have struggled hard to exclude all competition by women; and though the doctors have, from force of circumstances, been obliged to recognize lady practitioners, and though it is now possible for a woman both to obtain a thorough medical education and to set up in practice, it was most unwillingly that as much as this has been conceded. The legal profession still remains entirely closed, though some few lady conveyancers find means of earning a livelihood. It is readily admitted that some occupations are specially suitable to men as others are to women; but it is most unnecessary when natural causes are sure to intervene and restrict certain employments to one sex only, that men should enforce artificial restrictions that are not judiciously or justly conceived.

It would be childish to imagine that had women votes their wages would immediately rise to the level of men's; the causes of the existing differences of remuneration are of too varied and complex a nature to allow of any solution so simple. But there is little doubt that enfranchisement would place them in a better position for making terms with their employers, that it would encourage the independence that does not shrink from seeking work far a-field, and that such restrictions as are really found necessary for the regulation of labour would be enforced with their sanction and concurrence.

The jealousy that exists among male bread-winners, at what they call the intrusion of women, should be dissipated by the thought that every woman who earns her own livelihood, saves some man the labour of earning it for her.

Before leaving the subject of women's grievances, it will be as well to say a few words in order to correct the impression that women regard a seat in Parliament as a desirable attainment, and count their exclusion from it in

WOMEN'S GRIEVANCES.

the list of their grievances. Women do not look upon a seat in Parliament as a principle to be fought for. They have observed that the working men of England have managed to get their wishes attended to without direct representation; and, valuable as working-men members have proved themselves to be in the House of Commons when legislating on labour questions, it is probable that as much would have been done for the classes they represent had they failed to secure election. <u>It is the vote that has made citizens of the working men, and it is the vote that is worth fighting for as representing a great principle.</u>

At the same time, the rights of constituencies to return whom they will to serve them in the House of Commons should be respected; and were a woman to be found particularly fitted for the position, and a constituency, whether composed of men only, or of men and women together, chose to elect her, women would certainly accept the duty willingly, and stand up for their right to serve. But they wish it to be understood that it is not for this that they are agitating, as they look upon the franchise as a far more important object to be attained. This point should be specially emphasized, as it is constantly supposed that this is the main object of the agitation, and that were votes granted the other would necessarily follow. But there is no compulsion on Parliament ever to go farther than it chooses.

For similar reasons it is seldom that in England the expression "Women's Rights" is heard from the advocates of this movement. "Women's Suffrage" or "The Franchise for Women" is much more constantly made use of, as it defines with far greater exactitude what is being aimed at. They believe that the franchise is the key to the whole question, the real solution of the difficulty, and that once that is secured, any other rights, that have justice and equity to recommend them, will be naturally and easily secured. "Women's Rights" is a vague, indefinite term, apt to frighten unnecessarily the more timid spirits, while "Women's Suffrage" expresses clearly what is asked for, and is certainly the more satisfactory expression.

CHAPTER VII.

RIGHTS ALREADY OBTAINED.

It is perhaps as well to state what political privileges women already possess, as it seems but a small step farther in the same direction to give them the parliamentary vote.

Women householders vote for Boards of Guardians throughout Great Britain, but, as is well known, the voting papers are distributed and afterwards collected at the houses of the voters, so that no visit to the polling-booth is necessary. Qualified women can and do sit as Guardians of the Poor in Great Britain, but not in Ireland.[1]

Women householders vote for school-board members wherever School Boards have been established, but as the Education Act has not been extended to Ireland, here also women are without a vote. Women, whether married or single, may be elected to serve as members of School Boards.

Women householders have votes for municipal coun-

[1] See Appendix XII.

cils in all incorporated towns in Great Britain, with the exception of London, which remains at present unreformed. In no case, however, do women sit as Town Councillors. In both the school-board and municipal elections, it is necessary to vote at the polling-place. It is well to draw attention to this fact, as a suggestion has lately been made, that should women be granted the parliamentary franchise, it would be necessary to make some special arrangement by which they might record their votes without visiting the polling-places. When it is considered that large numbers of women vote already without inconvenience, such care for their safety seems superfluous. Women would desire uniformity in these smaller electoral matters also.

As married women are found useful on School Boards, it seems curious that they should have so much difficulty in qualifying for Boards of Guardians, as their knowledge of children and the management of households would be of special use in fitting them to look after the large pauper schools and the internal arrangements of the workhouses. Ireland should also be put on an equal footing with Great Britain. Women feel certain that any future municipal reform laws will include them, as when, not long since (1882), a reform of municipalities in Scotland took place, women householders were for the first time enfranchised without the smallest discussion in either House of Parliament. It was done as a matter of course.

The Irish Municipal Franchise Bill, that has several

times lately been unsuccessfully introduced, follows the Scotch Bill in assimilating the municipal franchise of Ireland to that of Great Britain, both as regards women voters and other matters. There are some few Boards in Ireland, such as the Belfast Harbour Commissioners and the Town Commissioners in several places, for which women have votes ; but otherwise the women of Ireland are treated in voting matters in a much worse manner than their English sisters, and there is an attempt being made at this present time to prevent them from voting even for these Boards.

Women have occasionally received appointments from the Government in the shape of inspectorships ; and in 1884 three ladies were appointed by the Local Government Board to sit as members of the Metropolitan Asylums Board. But as these posts depend on the good-will of the President of the Local Government Board, they are not numerous, and cannot be counted on as a right. However, as women take their place more conspicuously in political life, and it is recognized more widely what good special work they are able to perform, it is to be hoped that these appointments will become more frequent.

It is well known that some of the public offices are open to women, and that large numbers earn their livelihood as clerks, telegraphists, and mistresses of post-offices. Public school teachers also constitute a large body of women, but these occupations hardly come within the category of political rights, although they show that there is no hesitation in making use of women as public servants.

The constituencies have lately shown themselves in advance of Members of Parliament, by including women in the various political organizations that now exist in every constituency. In some few cases a rule exists that the persons forming the Liberal Association, or Caucus, must be voters, but this has been got over in some instances by the fact that women are municipal voters; and in most associations any subscriber to the funds is a qualified person, so that there is no exclusion on the ground of sex. But these associations have gone farther, and elected women to serve on the Councils, that is to say, the bodies that select the parliamentary candidates to bring forward at the elections. Among Conservatives the prominence given to women as Dames of the Primrose League, is another important recognition of their political value.

CHAPTER VIII.

A LIMITED DEMAND FOR JUSTICE.

HAVING carefully stated the various arguments advanced in favour of Women's Suffrage, it is necessary to consider the different proposals that are made for giving women votes.

There are no less than three. There are some persons who make direct for universal suffrage, not, as the word is constantly used, to mean manhood suffrage, but literally "universal suffrage" for men and women alike.

Others, again, wish to make voting depend on a property qualification, that could be held by either married or unmarried women, especially as, since the passing of the Married Women's Property Act of 1882, wives can hold property in their own right.

Thirdly, there are the advocates of an extension of the franchise to unmarried women and widows only, following as a precedent the laws relating to the local franchises. It will be necessary to say a few words on each of these proposals.

In countries like the United States, where universal

suffrage exists already for men, there is only one logical platform to occupy, and that is to demand similar rights for women. Anything short of this would be to give up the fundamental principle of equality before the law for both sexes. But in England the position is different. Men have not got universal suffrage, and it would of course be quite impossible to ask for women what men have not yet got. It remains, then, for the advocates of this great and sweeping change to work for the extension to all men and women alike of the franchise.

This is hardly an encouraging task, and but few have seriously undertaken it. In England we have such an engrained habit of going step by step, and even of experimenting in legislation, that it seems quite hopeless to suppose that an English House of Commons would go in for as much as this all at once. What is feared by the advocates of Women's Suffrage is, that by hastening the passing of universal suffrage they would only see manhood suffrage become law, and undoubtedly their position in that case would be worse than it now is. The most logical work to be done seems, therefore, to be, to place women who are qualified as the law now stands, on an equality with men, in the hope that when the day of universal suffrage arrives, men will have had experience to a limited extent of the political capacities of women, and the experiment having proved a successful one, they will be ready to extend the right to all alike. Women have entire confidence in such an experiment, and feel no doubt of its success.

A LIMITED DEMAND FOR JUSTICE.   89

It is so difficult to tell when a question in England will become practical, and not merely theoretical, that it is impossible to predict whether universal suffrage is likely to be reached in the next decade or in the next century. If not for a hundred years, then is the argument all the more urgent for making household suffrage complete at the present time. Besides, the moment you advocate votes for all, it becomes necessary to face the important argument that in the British Isles the women out-number the men by nearly a million, and that therefore all power would be placed in their hands. It does not do to insist too much on the cogency of this line of reasoning, as under the ballot it would be impossible to find out whether the women had out-voted the men or not; but it is a fact that carries weight with many minds, and if, by enfranchising only a limited number of women, the position can be turned altogether, it would certainly seem advisable to do so.

In the United States, as in all newly colonized countries, the men are numerically a larger body than the women, so they are not obliged to take this factor into consideration.

It is not at all impossible that in the United Kingdom the question of universal suffrage may be indefinitely postponed, for there has always been a strong bias in this country in favour of a property or occupation qualification for voting purposes. If, then, the proposal to obtain universal suffrage is set on one side as either impracticable or impolitic, the question that has to be settled is where to draw the line. Is it easiest and best to draw the line between the married and unmarried women, or is it preferable to make it entirely a question of property, and not allow marriage to have anything to do with the matter? It will be easily seen that this is much more a matter of expediency than of principle, although it is a point that is being very hotly debated at the present time.

It is known that a large number of men are ready to vote, and are pledged to vote, for the extension of the suffrage to unmarried women and widows, while they have insuperable prejudices against allowing any wives at all to vote. It is therefore probable that it would be possible to pass one Bill through the Houses of Parliament at once, while the other would have to face much stronger opposition.[1]

Every man, be he Member of Parliament, or be he an ordinary citizen, who looks upon himself as the supreme head of his household, and refuses to admit the modern theory that the best marriages are founded on a system of equality or partnership, is certain to vote against any proposal to enfranchise his wife, even in exceptional cases. To a person of average intelligence the line is much clearer between the married and unmarried women than if drawn in any other place. It is the same line that already exists with regard to the local franchises, so that it has all the force of precedent on its side.

It has been thought by many persons that the

[1] See Appendix XIII.

passing of the Married Women's Property Act had so altered the position of wives, had placed them legally in so independent a position, that the rights obtained for unmarried women would, as, a matter of course, extend to them. Accordingly many attempted to vote in the following municipal elections, but in every case their vote was disallowed as soon as proof was given of a living husband. Had they been able to vote, it would have only been logical to include them in the claim for the parliamentary franchise, but as they are shown to be disqualified by marriage, it seems better and wiser to restrict the demand to the unmarried women and widows. The hardship to these latter is much greater of remaining unrepresented, and their enfranchisement does not raise the question of political division in the family and consequent disagreement.

The woman who earns her own living, or is mistress of her own household, may be no better or wiser or more capable of exercising a vote than her married sister—indeed it is probable that taken all round there is not much to choose in these respects between the two; but it is quite certain that her vote will be more independent, and that she will give it more in accordance with her own judgment.

To return to the analogy with slaves, which, after all, is the truest, it would be impossible to give votes to slaves as long as they were in a state of servitude: set them free first, and then grant them votes as quickly as may be afterwards. So it is difficult to imagine that English married women, with their very children held as hostages for their obedience and submission, could give an unbiassed vote were it granted them. The day of their freedom is not far off, and will be immensely hastened by the voting power of their freer sisters; but even the Married Women's Property Act, beneficial as have been its provisions, is only one strand cut of the rope that binds them, that too being an Act of far greater importance to the rich than to the poor.

All Bills and Resolutions brought into the House of Commons previous to 1884 were ambiguously worded, as none of the friends of the movement wished to exclude married women in so many words, as many urged that it would prove a bar to their future enfranchisement. This was all very well as long as the question was considered a theoretical rather than a practical one. But when in 1884 large offers of support were made by the Conservative party, it was found absolutely necessary to define it one way or another. The decision was certainly influenced by the speech of the then Attorney-General, Sir Henry James, in which he declared that were the Bill passed in a form admitting a certain number of married women, it would encourage the fabrication of numerous faggot-votes, wealthy husbands bestowing on their wives just sufficient property to qualify them for a vote, and that the legislature should not be a party to such manufacture of votes.

The Women's Suffrage Society did not exactly take

this view of the question, as they firmly believed that their resolutions only referred to unmarried women, as only they were really qualified. They do not therefore admit that by inserting in 1884 the words, "Provided that nothing in this Act contained shall enable women under coverture to be registered or to vote at such elections," they disenfranchised one woman who would otherwise have been enabled to vote. They had for some time felt that by allowing this ambiguity to continue, they were laying themselves open to a charge of dishonesty, of attempting to smuggle in a certain number of married women without the public really comprehending that they were doing so. As they had never any intention of including married women, they considered it judicious to remove all doubt on the point.

There are many firm friends of Women's Suffrage who think that could a Bill be framed admitting but one woman to vote, and that Bill could be passed at once, while a more comprehensive measure would have to wait longer, it would be advisable to take even that small boon, as it would carry a great principle along with it. This may be a somewhat extreme form of "opportunism," but the proverb is undoubtedly true in politics as elsewhere, "that half a loaf is better than no bread," only in politics it is advisable to add the proviso, that the acceptance of the half-loaf can never preclude the starving from afterwards attempting to obtain more.

It seems obvious that the difference of opinion on

this question should not cause any serious division among the political friends of women, as it is a fair point for discussion in Committee of the House of Commons, when it will be clearly seen what it is possible to obtain at once and what is impossible.

If married women were be included no one would rejoice so much as the Women's Suffrage Society which supports the other course. There is no feeling of antagonism on their part to the admission of any person to the franchise, but as a matter of tactics they have considered it wiser not to "deck load" their Bill. By the provisions of the Bill they promoted, it is calculated that about 800,000 persons would be able to be registered as voters at once, which though not a formidable addition to the electorate compared to the most recent, is yet a very large number to leave without due protection or representation.

The number of women householders varies apparently very considerably in different localities, and is naturally greater in the more well-to-do communities. For instance, it was ascertained in May, 1885, that in the Queen's Park Estate of the Artizan Dwellings Company in the Harrow Road, 6½ per cent. of the householders were women. This is lower than in most districts, but it is obvious that in dwellings specially designed for artizans there would be a tendency to let them, in the first instance at any rate, to working men rather than to women.

A LIMITED DEMAND FOR JUSTICE.   95

In other districts of London it has been found that no less than 15 per cent. of the householders are women. This is very much nearer the mark, as in 1871, according to the return of municipal electors in the various incorporated towns of England and Wales, exclusive of London, which still remains unreformed, it was found that more than 108,000 women possessed the municipal franchise, being in the proportion of 16 per cent. of the municipal voters. It is doubtful whether the counties and non-incorporated towns could show so many independent women, but 15 per cent. may well be accepted as the most accurate figure.

Admitting that all women cannot vote, and therefore that, at first, a selection, more or less arbitrary, must represent the rest, one of the reasons for drawing the distinction between married and unmarried women is that it would take women from all the classes that now furnish male voters. It would be impossible to say that it was specially designed to include one class of women and exclude another, that it was for the rich and not for the poor.

It would include women owning land, whether vast estates obtained by inheritance, or some few acres cultivated by the exertions of their own family. The Return of Owners of Land in 1872, popularly called the New Domesday Book, gives the number of women landowners of one acre and upwards in England and Wales as 37,806 out of 269,547—a proportion of one in seven. In Ireland the proportion of women landowners is somewhat less, being one in eight. Women farmers, though a decreasing body in Great Britain, yet number as many as 22,000 in England and Wales alone, so that, by including Scotland, the number cannot be very far short of 30,000.[1] Across the Irish Channel, where the holdings are so much smaller and therefore more easily managed by a woman, the number is very much greater, and has by some persons been placed as high as 60,000. All these would obtain votes.

Then the women who earn their livelihood in some profession, whether lady doctors, or in the various branches of the teaching profession, would be numerously represented. The women owning shops or carrying on businesses of every description, from the big manufacturer to the laundry woman, sensibly swell the roll. And even the working women, provided they were thrifty enough to qualify themselves, would find a place in these 800,000. As the last census [2] shows, with more than three million of women earning their own livelihood—a considerable increase on previous figures—the number of female householders is probably growing larger.

Were married women with property of their own to be enfranchised, they would certainly not be found among a poorer class of women than have just been named, though an attempt has been made to claim for such a measure a more popular basis than for the other. It is hardly realized by some who urge that the best women of the nation are being left on one side, what a large

---

[1] See Appendix XIV.   [2] See Appendix XV.

number of widows there are among these householders, women who have had all the experience of marriage, and, besides that, the responsibility that must always rest on the head of the house.

There is a question of minor importance to that of the inclusion or exclusion of married women that is yet constantly discussed, and certainly cannot be omitted from the controversy. This is the question of the lodger vote. If the franchise is to follow on the same lines as those laid down for men, there is no question but that women lodgers must be included. If, on the other hand, it is extended merely to those women who already enjoy the right to vote at all local elections, the lodger question does not arise. But this would be to relinquish altogether the principle that has been fought for.

Undoubtedly, to enfranchise lodgers, would be to place a vote in the hands of some of the least worthy of their sex, and there seem to be many persons who imagine that no sooner does a woman live in lodgings than her right to the name of an honest woman following a moral and praiseworthy calling is at once relinquished, and she has no business to imagine she has the same claim to a vote as a woman householder.[1] In the first place, to exclude women lodgers, on the ground of the immorality of a certain number among them, would be a gross injustice to the remainder. Secondly, it would be setting up a code of morality for one sex not enforced against the

[1] See Appendix XVI.

other, a principle which has already been protested against in these pages, for the question of the morality of male-voters has never even been discussed in considering the question of enfranchisement. It is quite impossible, when votes are to be granted, to draw distinctions that will include all that is virtuous and exclude all that is vicious. If confined to women householders alone, a certain number of the very class sought to be excluded would be given votes, and even marriage could not be considered an absolute guarantee of character. On the other hand, by the exclusion of the woman lodger, a hard-working, meritorious class of women would not only be shut out, but stigmatized most undeservedly, and Women Suffrage would become still more than among men a luxury for the rich rather than a defence for the poor. It is possible that the Legislature may choose to mutilate the Bill in this respect, but it is impossible to imagine that women would be a party to it.

The tendency is becoming greater in our towns, and in London especially, to build large blocks of houses let out in flats or even in single rooms, so that the number of persons occupying an entire house does not increase at the same rate as the population. But these all come under the heading of separate tenements, carrying with them the household vote, so that, although the lodger-vote includes an important and hardworking section of the population, it is not increasing as much as the ordinary observer might suppose. Its exclusion would not disfranchise the nomadic portion of the population any more than is already done by household suffrage ; but in any case, women claim in this matter also equality with men, and consider that by so doing they are ensuring the most equable and lasting adjustment of the question.

The numerous points of interest and importance bearing more or less directly on the question of female emancipation can hardly be touched on in these pages. Among men it is found injurious and debilitating, mentally and morally to both sides, for one set of persons to be in complete subjection to another ; and if they could only be persuaded that the same thing applies to women, they might realize that it is not for the public weal that such a state of things should continue.

Women have good reason to claim, that whereas the eighteenth century saw the awakening of men to enlightenment and self-improvement, the nineteenth century has seen a yet greater change in the condition and education of women. They have already reduced the intellectual distance between the sexes, but are fearful lest, without some direct encouragement such as enfranchisement would give, the enthusiasm for progress may die away—at any rate be seriously checked and retarded.

While agitating for an improvement in their political condition, they have not only confined their energies to strictly constitutional methods, but have endeavoured to keep clear of the more tortuous paths of political intrigue, believing their cause to be sufficiently strong to stand on its own merits. They have also considered it more judicious to stand aloof from all other movements, be they religious, political, or social, even should a large proportion of the members of the Society approve of any such movement.

The ultimate political equality of the sexes is their aim and object, and they are willing gratefully to accept the help and assistance of persons of both sexes, and all creeds and political beliefs, while at the same time committing themselves as a whole to no other platform than Women's Suffrage. Ignorance and prejudice are, they believe, the two giants in the pathway to be overcome, and so sure are they of the logic and justice of their cause, that if ignorance on the subject can be entirely removed, prejudice must succumb without a struggle.

APPENDICES.

APPENDICES.

APPENDIX I.

REPLY OF *Mr. Disraeli* TO THE MEMORIAL ON WOMEN'S SUFFRAGE, APRIL 29, 1873.

"DEAR GORE LANGTON,—I was much honoured by receiving from your hands the memorial signed by 11,000 women of England, among them some illustrious names, thanking me for my services in attempting to abolish the anomaly that the parliamentry franchise attached to a household or property qualification, when possessed by a woman, should not be exercised, though in all matters of local government, when similarly qualified, she exercises this right. As I believe this anomaly to be injurious to the best interests of the country, I trust to see it removed by the wisdom of Parliament.—Yours sincerely,
"B. DISRAELI."

APPENDIX II.

SPEECH OF *Sir Stafford Northcote* IN THE HOUSE OF COMMONS.

ON the final debate before the second reading of the Reform Bill, April 7th, 1884, Sir Stafford Northcote said:—
"If you make a capable elector the test, you will find that

you are bound to go very much further and in very different directions in some respects to what you have done in order to complete your definition. I take the case of the female franchise. There cannot be a doubt, if you ask who are capable electors, you would find it very difficult to declare that the females who are in a certain position as taxpayers and ratepayers, and who are electors for municipal purposes, are not capable citizens, and that they should not be included in the franchise. I believe that about one-seventh of the electors of the municipalities of the kingdom are females, and on the principle on which you are proceeding you will find it difficult to say that they are not entitled to vote."

APPENDIX III.

In the Women's Suffrage Debate, June, 1884, *Mr. Joseph Cowen* said:—

"Some hon. members have argued that the domestic arena is the only one for which women are qualified, but they exhibit great ignorance and great forgetfulness of history. Our parasitic conventionalities, our fantastic and fanciful modes of life, while professing to honour women, degrade them. Our very homage contains a latent irony. It stimulates to cultivation of woman's personal graces and lighter accomplishments, and to the neglect of her nobler powers. We surround her with a world of dolls, and then complain that she is frivolous. We deprive her of the lessons and stimulus of practical outdoor life, and then we chide her with being flippant and undisciplined. But notwithstanding these disadvantages the number of women who have shone as sovereigns, or who have risen to renown in politics, literature, art, and ordinary life, has been exceptionally large. Call the roll of the most distinguished rulers the world has known—keep in mind the predominance of man over woman—and will any one contend that the proportion of great queens has not been in excess of the great kings? The three brightest eras in British history have been those in which the sceptre has been swayed by a woman—those of Elizabeth, Anne, and Victoria. What does Austria owe to Maria Theresa, Sweden to the valiant daughter of Gustavus Adolphus, and Spain to Isabella, who pawned her jewels to fit out a fleet for Columbus? Can any one, in face of such instances, gainsay the fact that, the opportunity being given, woman, in spite of her artificial training, has risen to the responsibilities of rulership? But hon. members have argued that one of the first qualifications of a citizen was to be able to fight, and that, as women cannot act as soldiers or policemen, they cannot therefore be electors—that as they cannot build ships nor make guns, nor lead armies, they should therefore be deprived of their civil rights. Do we disfranchise men because they are below the military standard? Are the weak, the aged, and the failing eliminated from the register? Is it fair to apply to woman a test we do not apply to man? We refuse to allow her to take a share in the work of the world. The enervating habits we have imposed on her have impaired her physical powers, and then we cite to her detriment the weakness which our customs have created. Men with splendid natural endowments often die mute and inglorious for want of discipline and opportunity. Great commanders grow out of the circumstances in which their lives are cast. Open to woman the same scenes, immerse her in the same great pursuits and interests, and, if she fails, then, but not till then, shall we be able to make a basis of argument against her on the ground of intellectual incapacity. Those hon. members who use this fighting argument forget the martial energy of the Scandinavian women. When my hon. friend the member for Stoke (Mr. Woodall) mentioned the names of Boadicea and Joan of Arc a titter went round among hon. members, who in their hurried march of executive life have allowed reflection to be submerged by locomotion, thought by action, and ideality by a narrow and soulless materialism. But the names of the gifted and the lost will live, and the lessons of their lives will stir the pulses of mankind when all our petty politics are forgotten."

APPENDIX IV.

Mr. Herbert Spencer ON WOMEN'S SUFFRAGE.

"THE extension of the law of equal freedom to both sexes will doubtless be objected to on the ground that the political privileges exercised by men must thereby be ceded to women also. Of course they must; and why not? . . . We are told, however, that 'woman's mission' is a domestic one, that her character and position do not admit of her taking part in the decision of public questions—that politics are beyond her sphere. But this raises the question, Who shall say what her sphere is? . . . As the usages of mankind vary so much, let us hear how it is to be shown that the sphere *we* assign her is the true one—that the limits *we* have set to female activity are just the proper limits. Let us hear why on this point of our social polity we are exactly right, whilst we are wrong on so many others. We must conclude that, being required by that first pre-requisite to greatest happiness, the law of equal freedom, such a concession is unquestionably right and good."

APPENDIX V.

IN an article entitled "Women's Suffrage and the Franchise Bill," that appeared in *The Pall Mall Gazette*, January 14, 1884, *Mrs. Henry Fawcett* says :—

"I believe it will one day be considered almost incredible that there ever was a time when the idea of giving votes to women who fulfil the conditions which enable men to vote was regarded as dangerous and revolutionary. There is nothing apparently more subversive of reason and judgment than fear. The Duke of Wellington was afraid of the Reform Bill of 1832, and honestly believed that it would bring down in general ruin property, the Crown, and the Church. Some of the most astute men of the world of the pre-Reform era were misled in a similar way. The author of the 'Greville Memoirs,' writing in 1831 of the scene in the House of Lords, when William IV. dissolved Parliament, speaks of the king with the 'tall, grim figure of Lord Grey close beside him with the Sword of State in his hand; it was as if the king had got his executioner by his side, and the whole picture looked strikingly typical of his and our future destinies.' The day for these extravagant hallucinations has passed. As Mr. Bright said some time ago in speaking of household suffrage in Irish boroughs: 'Men are afraid of the first experiment of something which has a dangerous appearance; but if they find that their fears were altogether imaginary, they make a second experiment without fear.' Some people seemed at one time to think that the whole order of society, the very laws of nature, would be reversed if household suffrage were made to include women; but a first experiment has been made in giving women the municipal and school-board suffrages. The fears at first expressed have proved altogether imaginary; society has not been turned upside down; the possession of a vote has not made women essentially different from what they were before; we still like needlework; we prefer pretty gowns to ugly ones; we are interested in domestic management and economy, and are not altogether indifferent to our friends and relations; and we ask, therefore, that a second experiment should be made without fear."

APPENDIX VI.

WOMEN'S SUFFRAGE IN THE MIDDLE AGES.

"THERE are extant many parliamentary returns for counties and boroughs from the earliest times which were made by female electors, and yet were received. Some of these are enumerated in Prynne's collection of parliamentary writs, some of later date are mentioned in the Commons Journals themselves, others are to be found in the repositories of the learned or the curious."

"In the reign of Elizabeth there had happened several elections to Parliament for a borough (the more than once famous borough of Aylesbury), where the franchise was then claimed and exercised by a simple family of 'inhabitants,' and long continued to be so claimed and exercised. Now at one of those elections, the 'sole elector being a minor,' his mother *jure repræsentationis*, had actually voted in his stead —elected two burgesses—signed their indenture—and as returning officer made the following return, which was upheld as good :—

"'To all Christian people to whom this present writing shall come, I, Dame Dorothy Packington, widow, late wife of Sir John Packington, knight, lord, and owner of the town of Aylesbury, sendeth greeting : know ye *me*, the said Dame Dorothy Packington, to have *chosen, named, and appointed* my trusty and well-beloved Thomas Lichfield and John Burden, Esquires, to be *my burgesses*, of *my said town of Aylesbury*. And whatsoever the said Thomas and John, burgesses, shall do in the service of the queen's highness in that present Parliament, to be holden at Westminster, the 8th day of May next ensuing the date hereof, I, the same Dame Dorothy Packington, do ratify and approve to be my own act, *as fully and wholly as if I were or might be present there*. In witness,'" etc.—"On some supposed Constitutional Restraints upon the Parliamentary Franchise," by *Mr. Chisholm Anstey.*

APPENDIX VII.

Mr. Gladstone ON THE WOMEN'S DISABILITIES REMOVAL BILL, 1871.

"THE ancient law recognized the rights of women in the parish; I apprehend they could both vote and act in the parish. The modern rule has extended the right to the municipality, so far as the right of voting is concerned. . . . With respect to School Boards, I own I believe that we have done wisely, on the whole, in giving both the franchise and the right of sitting on the School Board to women. Then comes a question with regard to Parliament, and we have to ask ourselves whether we shall or shall not go farther. . . . I admit, at any rate, that as far as I am able to judge, there is more presumptive ground for change in the law than some of the opponents of the measure are disposed to own. . . . I cannot help thinking that, for some reason or other, there are various important particulars in which women obtain much less than justice under social arrangements. . . . I may be told that there is no direct connection between this and the parliamentary franchise, and I admit it ; but, at the same time, I am by no means sure that these inequalities may not have an indirect connection with a state of law in which the balance is generally cast too much against women, and too much in favour of men. There is one instance which has been quoted, and I am not sure there is not something in it—I mean the case of farms. . . . I believe to some extent in the competition for that particular employment women suffer in a very definite manner in consequence of their want of qualification to vote. I go somewhat further than this, and say that, so far as I am able to form an opinion of the general tone and colour of our law in these matters, where the peculiar relation of men and women are concerned, that law does less than justice to women, and great mischief, misery, and scandal result from that state of things in many of the occurrences and events of life. . . . If it should be found possible to arrange a safe and well-adjusted alteration of the law as to political power, the man who shall attain the object, and who shall see his purpose carried onward to its consequences in a more just arrangement of the provisions of other laws bearing upon the condition and welfare of women, will, in my opinion, be a real benefactor to his country.—*Speech in the House of Commons, May* 3, 1871.

APPENDIX VIII.

At the Town Hall, Shoreditch, on October 13, 1884, in the course of his speech *Mr. Fawcett* said:—

"Search through the speeches that have been delivered in favour of the enfranchisement of the rural householder, and I say there is not an argument or an appeal that has been made which does not bring into striking relief the injustice of saying that no woman shall be admitted to any share in the government of her country. How often have we heard it said, ' Be just and fear not ? ' Does this maxim apply only to men ! On a thousand platforms we have declared that taxation and representation should go together, we have denounced the injustice that if war is being waged the agricultural labourer should have a portion of his hard-won earnings taken from him without any power of expressing his opinion on the policy for which he is taxed. Is it more just that women should be taxed without their consent? Have they a less severe struggle for existence ? Are their earnings so much more easily won that increased taxation means for them a less keenly felt sacrifice ? There is not a subject which is discussed in Parliament in which women are not as deeply interested as men. War not only brings to them its burdens, but it often brings the sorrow and the anguish of a desolated home ; the widowed mother may be made childless, the sister may mourn a brother who will be seen no more. Social questions are probably likely to engage an increasing share of the attention of Parliament, and is there any social question in which women are not deeply concerned ? Education is not a less priceless blessing to them than it is to men. If the Church is to be disestablished—the very intensity of the interest which you manifest shows that wishes of women on such a question are entitled to the fullest consideration. If restrictions are imposed on their employment, are they to be deprived of all power of resistance if they believe that fresh difficulties will be thus thrown in the way of a woman earning her living by honest toil? I have said I think it is not less expedient than it is just that the claim of women to vote should be considered on its merits. I well remember Mr. Henley, who was the very embodiment of shrewd common sense, at the time when the Liberal party was involved in a labyrinth of proposals about a £6 rating and a £7 rental franchise, said, 'Why don't you go to household suffrage at once? You will have to go there sooner or later, and sooner is better than later.' These were the words of a Conservative, but they were the words of wisdom and sagacity. Depend upon it that the claim of women householders to vote will be so irresistible when the suffrage has been conferred upon every man who is a householder, however poor and uneducated he may be, that I believe the demand of women householders to be enfranchised will not rest until it is conceded. You will have to do it sooner or later, and sooner is better than later. No one who watches the signs of the times can doubt that this demand will not alone be urged by women. As illustrating the amount of popular feeling in its favour, I may refer to the fact that at so representative a gathering of working men as the Trades' Union Congress, a resolution in support of Women's Suffrage was, much to their credit, a few weeks since passed with only three dissentients."

APPENDIX IX.

The Bishop of Carlisle ON WOMEN'S SUFFRAGE.

"WHILE the number of voters was comparatively small, I consider that those voters were trustees for the general population. This was pre-eminently the case before the first Reform Bill, but it continued to be so after that Bill had become law; there could be no justification of the principle of giving a vote to £10 householders and not to poorer folks, except the assumption that a vote implied a trust to be exercised by the better-educated and more substantial class for the good of all. While this was the principle of legislation, I consider that there was no wrong committed in not permitting women to vote; the question was simply one of the extent of a trust, and my own opinion used to be that, upon the whole, women were happier and the government of the country better carried on without the admission of women into the political arena. When, however, the arbitrary £10 line was done away with, and the borough franchise made to extend to every man who had anything which could be fairly called a home, this view of trusteeship was immensely weakened, and, as soon as the vote is extended beyond boroughs, as undoubtedly it will be, I consider that the notion of a man as a voter holding a trust for his neighbours will be well-nigh exploded altogether. I do not say that a vote will not be, in any case, a trust, and an important one, but this will not be its chief characteristic; it is inconceivable that it should be. Consequently, the question of female suffrage assumes, to my mind, an aspect which it never had before. If a woman be a householder, still more if she be an employer of labour and one through whose employment a number of men possess votes, what is there in the mere accident of sex to make it right to say she shall have no political influence? I do not in the least desire that married women should vote. This seems to me undesirable and impossible. The husband and wife must be one in this as in other things. But when the woman satisfies every condition but that of sex, then it seems to me impossible in reason, and I believe it will soon be impossible in fact, to deprive her of a vote. These, in brief, are the opinions which I hold on the subject of female suffrage.—Believe me, yours sincerely,

"*August* 9, 1884."   "H. CARLISLE.

APPENDIX X.

The Master of the Rolls, in giving judgment in the *Agar-Ellis Case*, said:—

AGAR-ELLIS CASE.

" By the law of England *the father* has control over the person and education and condition of his children until they attain twenty-one years. It is also the law of England that if any one alleges that another is under illegal control, he may apply for a writ of *habeas corpus*, and have the person so controlled brought up before the Court. The question for the Court is whether the person is in illegal custody without that person's consent. Now up to a certain age infant children cannot consent or withhold consent. They can object or they can submit, but they cannot consent. The law as a general rule has fixed on a certain age, in the case of a boy at fourteen, and in the case of a girl at sixteen, up to which the Court will not, upon an application for *habeas corpus* as between father and child, inquire as to whether the child does or does not consent to remain in the place where it may be. But after that age the Court will inquire, and if it should be ascertained that the infant, no longer a child, is consenting to remain in the place where it is, then the point for granting a *habeas corpus* fails. His lordship, after observing that the same law was now administered by all the judges, said that the cases referred to as to the writ of *habeas corpus* did not at all apply to the propositions for which they were cited. In the present case, of course, they had no application, as this young lady was not away from her father, but under his control, and any order made upon this petition would be in effect against the father to remove her from his custody. Then, with respect to the testamentary guardian, he is a creature of law, and nature has nothing to do with him. The law of England *recognizes the rights of the father*, not as the guardian, but *because he is the father of his children*, and if recognized as their guardian merely, his rights would probably be limited. The father has greater rights than the testamentary guardian or any other guardian can have. The testamentary guardian is not called on to feel affection for his ward, he is not called on to forgive his ward, he is not called on to treat his ward with tenderness. He has not the rights of the father because he is not the father. *The rights of the father are recognized because he is the father;* his duties as a father are recognized because they are natural duties. The natural duties of a father are to treat his children with the utmost affection, and with infinite tenderness; to forgive his children for any slip whatever, and under all circumstances. None of these duties are duties of the testamentary guardian. The law recognizes these duties, from which, if a father breaks, he breaks from everything which nature calls upon him to do; and although the law may not be able to insist upon their performance, it is because the law recognizes them, and knows that in almost every case the natural feelings of the father will prevail. The law trusts that the father will perform his natural duties, and does not, and, indeed, cannot, inquire how they have been performed. *The right of the father thus recognized is not a guardian's, but a paternal right; the right of a father because he is a father, which is far higher than that of any guardian*, and this because the law reposes trust in the father that he will perform his natural duties. There are, no doubt, cases which show the limits of this doctrine. If the father, by his immoral conduct, has become a person unfit, in the eyes of every one, to perform his duties to his child, and to claim the rights of a father towards his child, then if the child be a ward of Court—for otherwise the Court has no jurisdiction whatever—in such cases the Court will interfere. So, also, if the father has allowed certain things to be done, and then, by capricious change of purpose, has ordered the contrary, to the injury of the child, the Court will not allow that capricious change of mind to take effect, though if the thing had been done originally, the Court could not have interfered. I am not prepared to say whether, *when the child is a ward of Court, and the conduct of the father is such as to exhaust all patience—such, for instance, as cruelty, or pitiless spitefulness carried to a great extent—the Court might not interfere. But such interference will be exercised* ONLY IN THE UTMOST NEED, AND IN MOST

EXTREME CASES. It is impossible to lay down the rule of the Court more clearly than has been done by Vice-Chancellor Bacon in the recent case of 'Re Plowley' (47 'L. T.,' N.S., 283). In saying that this Court, 'whatever be its authority or jurisdiction, *has no authority to interfere with the sacred right of a father over his own children*,' the learned Vice-Chancellor has summed up all that I intended to say. *The rights of the father are sacred rights because his duties are sacred;* but the rights of the testamentary guardian are legal rights, and legal rights only. *With those sacred rights the Court has not interfered, and will not interfere, unless the conduct of the father has been such as to give the Court that authority.* If the father has been guilty of gross immorality, so as to make it improper that he should be guardian of any child, or if he is influenced by wicked, causeless caprice, which must be detrimental to the interests of the child, then the Court will interfere to prevent contamination or injury."—*The Times*, July 23, 1883.

APPENDIX XI.

AT a meeting in St. James's Hall, London, on July 5th, *Professor Lindsay* said he had made it his business to know something about the condition of the poor in the great cities. Alluding to the labour laws, he said that women's labour was being crippled by laws which pressed very heavily upon them. The Factory Acts were gradually driving women out of the factories, and when they were passed, the Home Secretary of the day actually refused to receive deputations of working women because they had no votes behind them; but he received deputations of working men because they had votes. It concerned the whole of them that women should have behind them that political force which was needed to make the expression of their mind go home. Women were being driven to the verge of starvation by the action of the law. They must live, but the tendency of legislation was against woman's work. What did that mean? It meant making women sink down into a life of shame. In taking up this matter he felt that he was pleading for the working women. Women would never get their rights until they had votes, so that they could bring their influence to bear upon Members of Parliament.

APPENDIX XII.

Mr. Courtney, M.P., ON WOMEN'S SUFFRAGE.

"THIS is, I think, a strictly moderate and a Conservative proposition. It goes on that principle of politics which we all respect, since it proceeds from experience. We have tried it, and what are the results? Are they beneficial or are they the reverse? Are they advantageous, whether as regards the constitution of the boards so elected or the character of the women who form part of the constituency? If they have been beneficial, they are in favour of our going further. No one has said they have produced injurious effects in either direction. On those, then, who oppose the extension of the principle that has been so far successful, the burden is thrown of showing the ineligibility of women for the parliamentary franchise. I can conceive one reason why hon. members may refuse to give votes for women being members of this House. They themselves might be affected by the change. This is, however, a very small reason indeed, and I should like to know what is the real explanation of this singular anomaly that hon. members are ready to give women votes at elections in which those hon. members are not directly concerned, and yet they refuse them in cases where they are so concerned. I confess I should have thought that one of the most hazardous things possible was the giving women votes at elections for Boards of Guardians, except, perhaps, making them eligible for seats in the School Boards. One would have thought that the enfranchisement of women in respect of Boards of Guardians might have tended to thwart the operation of the Poor Law ; yet, as a matter of fact, a totally different result has been witnessed, and so successful has been the experiment of admitting women, and so charitably and admirably have they endeavoured to carry out the operations of the Poor Law, that the Local Government Board has used its power of nominating women as Guardians where they have not been elected. If we take the case of elections to the School Boards, I ask is there a single thing that is of more importance to the nation than the education of the democracy of the future? And yet we give women votes for School Boards, and allow them to be elected as members of those boards, because they have to do with the education of girls. In making women capable of sitting on School Boards we have supplied them with a strong argument in favour of this motion, for the work of the School Boards far transcends in importance the ordinary questions that come before us at general elections."—*Speech in the House of Commons, July 6, 1883.*

APPENDIX XIII.

Rev. Canon Kingsley ON WOMEN'S SUFFRAGE.

"EVERY man is bound to bear in mind that over this increasing multitude of 'spinsters,' of women who are either self-supporting, or desirous of so being, men have, by mere virtue of their sex, absolutely no rights at all. No human being has such a right over them, as the husband has (justly or unjustly) over the wife, or the father over the daughter living in his house. They are independent and self-supporting units of the State, owing to it exactly the same allegiance as, and neither more nor less than, men who have attained their majority. They are favoured by no privilege, indulgence, or exceptional legislation from the State, and they ask none. They expect no protection from the State save that protection for life and property which every man, even the most valiant, expects since the carrying of side-arms has gone out of fashion. They prove themselves daily, whenever they have simple fair play, just as capable as men of not being a burden to the State. They are, in fact, in exactly the same relation to the State as men. Why are similar relations, similar powers, and similar duties, not to carry with them similar rights? To this question the common sense and justice of England will have soon to find an answer. I have sufficient faith in that common sense and justice, when once awakened to face any question fairly, to anticipate what that answer will be."—Paper in *Macmillan's Magazine*, 1869.

APPENDIX XIV.

SPEECH OF *Lord John Manners* IN THE HOUSE OF COMMONS, MARCH 24, 1884.

THE Marquis of Hartington having formally moved the second reading of the Franchise Bill, Lord John Manners rose to criticise it. In the course of his speech he said:

"But we are told that, in addition to its simplicity, this Bill will abolish all electoral anomalies. The Bill as it stands bristles with anomalies. There is an anomaly under the present system, and what I want the House to consider is will that anomaly not be greatly increased by this Bill—I allude to the question of the female ratepayer. The present position of the female ratepayer with regard to the vote is anomalous. She votes for municipal, school-board, and poor-law elections, but she does not vote at parliamentary elections. That is the position. Now, take the case of one large and influential section of the female ratepayers—I mean female farmers. The census shows that in 1881 there were upwards of 20,000 female farmers in England. At the present moment not one of these has the vote for parliamentary purposes. But, then, the labourer whom she pays, whom she maintains, enables to live in his cottage, has no vote now; but pass this Bill, and what happens? Every carter, every ploughman, every hedger and ditcher, every agricultural labourer who receives wages from the female farmer, will have the privilege of exercising the vote; but the female farmer who pays the wages, who is so important a factor in the economy of the parish, will remain without a vote. Will you tell me that that anomaly will not be greatly increased, and the sense of it embittered to the female ratepayer whom you are going to treat in this cavalier manner."

APPENDIX XV.

FEMALE EMPLOYMENT IN ENGLAND.

"FEMALE employment now plays a very important part in English industries, and it is interesting to note the number of persons thus engaged and the variety of their occupations. But lest the figures connected with this subject and appearing in the census returns for 1871 and 1881 should appear to be misleading, we must indicate the differences which have been made in enumeration. For example: in 1871 there were 7,642,000 females assigned to various classified occupations, whereas in 1881, with a greatly increased population, the whole number given was only 3,304,000. This is due to the fact that in the former year there were included, under various heads, no fewer than 4,364,000 females who no longer appear as being engaged in labour on their own account. There were in England and Wales 3,883,000 wives and others engaged in household duties; 388,000 wives assisting their husbands in divers occupations; and 92,000 wives, daughters, and nieces of farmers, who figured in the agricultural class. After deducting these, there has been a great increase in the past ten years in the number of females engaged in various industries, while some entirely new classes of female labour have been created. In the Civil Service there are 3216 female officers and clerks, while the municipal and other local authorities furnish employment for 3017. There are 1660 women engaged as missionaries, Scripture readers, and itinerant preachers, and 3795 appear as nuns and sisters of charity. There are 100 law clerks, 2646 midwives, and 35,175 engaged in subordinate medical service, nurses, assistants, &c. In the profession of teacher, females have increased enormously, the schoolmistresses numbering 94,221, and teachers, professors, and lecturers, 28,605. There is thus an army of 122,846 women engaged in educational work. Female musicians and music-mistresses number 11,376; inn or hotel servants, 26,487; and domestic servants, 1,230,406. In hospitals and institutions there were, by the last return, 11,528 females engaged; in washhouses and baths, 176,679; and as charwomen, 92,474. Some items will cause considerable astonishment. For instance, there were no fewer than 5989 females engaged as commercial clerks; 171 as 'pointsmen' at level crossings; and 4179 as 'warehousemen.' There were 2228 females employed in the telegraph and telephone services; 20,614 farmers and graziers; and 40,346 engaged in agricultural employment. Female bookbinders numbered 10,592, exceeding the men. There were 1233 toymakers and dealers; 2074 needle-makers; and 2503 steel-pen manufacturers. It is not a little curious that there were 1388 women engaged in various ramifications of the building trade, while 2035 were engaged as harness and whip makers. In the artificial flower business there were 4461 females; 1887 were in the match and firework trade; and 8578 in the tobacco trade. There were 32,890 female lodging-house keepers; 12,728 in hotel and public-house service; and 3728 in the beer and cider manufacture. There were also 7633 female bakers; 13,051 pastry-cooks; 6855 greengrocers; and 26,422 ordinary grocers. In the woollen cloth manufacture the females numbered 8501; in the making of worsted stuffs, 63,801; in the silk goods manufacture, 39,694; and in the cotton goods manufacture, 302,367—in the three last-named industries greatly exceeding the males employed. A considerable number of women were employed in connection with the flax, lace, and fustian manufactures. Of workers and dealers in dress there were no fewer than 616,425. Female farriers numbered 3645; brush and broom makers, 4185; japanners, 1539; cane workers, &c., 2525; wood turners and box makers, 2595; paper makers, 8277; paper-box makers, &c., 8718; coal miners, 3099; lead miners, 1903; brick and tile makers, 2738; earthenware and glass manufacturers, 21,490. There were 25,722 women shopkeepers; 17,660 costermongers, &c.; 1278 pawnbrokers; and 1403 rag gatherers and dealers. Engaged as mechanics or labourers, but not further specified, there were 17,769 women; while considerable numbers were employed in the apparently unfeminine occupations of nail and tin making, metal burnishing, bolt, nut, rivet, and screw making. Altogether a large percentage of the female population of the country were engaged in some kind of active employment."—*Times.*

APPENDIX XVI.

IN the debate on Women's Suffrage in the House of Commons, June, 1884, *Colonel King-Harman* said:—

"The hon. member for Huddersfield (Mr. Leatham) used an argument which I think a most unworthy one, namely, that the franchise is not to be extended to women because, unhappily, in this country, as in all others, there are women of a degraded and debased class. Because there are 40,000 of them in this metropolis alone, the remaining women who are pure and virtuous are to be deprived of the power of voting. But will the hon. member guarantee that the 2,000,000 men the Bill proposes to enfranchise, and whom he is perfectly prepared to see enfranchised, shall be pure and perfectly moral men? Will he ensure that amongst these 2,000,000 men there are none who are living on the wages of sin of these unfortunate women? Will the hon.

member propose a clause to exclude from the franchise those men who lead into vice, and retain in vice and degradation, these unfortunate women? Will he exclude every man who seduces a poor girl and brings her into this miserable class? No; men may sin and be a power in the State, but when a woman sins, not only is she to have no power, but her whole sisterhood are to be excluded from it. I consider the argument used by the hon. member an unworthy one, and one which will not bear the test of examination."